*Presented
by the
Government of New Zealand*

the

SEVEN SEAS PUBLISHING PTY LIMITED, WELLINGTON, NEW ZEALAND

'neath mantle of rangi

Brian Enting

(ORIGINAL NEW ZEALAND)

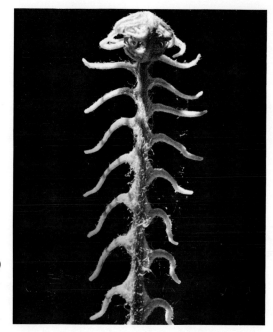

DEDICATED TO
HAROLD TREMBATH
AND HIS LATE WIFE ELSIE

acknowledgements

It is a pleasant task to express sincere thanks to my family and those people who have helped me with this project or accompanied me on my rambles. Special thanks go to:

Dr. Ian A. E. Atkinson, who, time after time, answered questions, identified plant species and helped in so many ways and to Miss Nancy M. Adams for her constructive comments on the manuscript. I also thank Dr. B. D. Bell, Mr. A. P. Druce, Mr. I. F. Grant, Mr. F. C. Kinsky, Mr. I. Hulse, Mr. G. G. Royle, Mr. D. L. N. Pidgeon, Mr. H. Sieben, Mr. A. H. Whitaker and the management and staffs of Mount Bruce, The National Museum and the Wildlife Division of the Department of Internal Affairs.

I would like to make it clear however that although these people have contributed valuable advice and opinions, I bear responsibility for the final content and any errors which it may contain.

ISBN 85467 036X

© 1976 Brian Enting
Seven Seas Publishing Pty Limited
Wellington, New Zealand

contents

foreword

Our slender country spans 13° of latitude, is little over 256 km wide at its broadest point and lies near the centre of the world's largest ocean. The climate varies from sub-tropical to sub-antarctic and most of the land in its virgin state was heavily forested. A high percentage of the land birds are unique and approximately ninety per cent of all the trees and shrubs occurring here grow on no other land.

There is still a lot to be learned about our various environments. At this time there are still many species of flowering plants to be named and botanists agree that there are more waiting to be discovered. Furthermore the sheer number of species means that no one person can achieve more than a passing knowledge of the plants or animals and their inter-relationships.

We have for instance many thousand native species of flowering plants, mosses, lichens, fungi, insects, birds, spiders, crustaceans, freshwater fish and land snails. This underlines the reliance and indebtedness which the amateur must acknowledge to the professionals in this field. Without their help, I would have been unable to find many species particularly the rarer ones and had little chance of accurate identification. To illustrate the complexities, a single plant can have different shaped leaves as juvenile compared with an adult, can vary from one part of the country to another, be a ground hugging plant in one situation or an erect shrub in another or to cap it all off, hybridise naturally to give numerous intermediate forms.

I set out to try to recreate photographically natural New Zealand as it was 100 years ago. The task proved impracticable to achieve completely, although I have got as close as is possible in the 1970's to achieving this goal. It is fortunate that there are a few remaining areas of truly virgin forest still left to illustrate how much has changed. The search for these remnants has taken me into forests, mountains, swamps, sand dunes, national parks and our only 'desert' the Rangipo, through all seasons. From this experience it seemed logical to present the results as found in each environment and thus share with the reader the impressions of each zone. Three broad divisions have been selected, coastal, lowland/montane, alpine and sub-alpine. Within each of these occur further divisions which I will cover briefly in the following pages.

Space and the economics of printing have limited content so that hundreds of photos have been eliminated and thousands of species ignored. The selection has been made on the basis of the appropriateness to the environment being discussed and on pictorial appeal. Not everyone wants to delve deeply into the literature of natural history. For those who do, an abbreviated bibliography appears at the end of the book and for those who don't, I hope that this book will take you one step closer to enjoying our natural heritage.

Our land is still being shaped and the plants and animals continue to evolve. Now however we face a changing environment in which a new balance between the native and introduced elements has still to be reached. It is likely that the new balance will produce a flora and fauna markedly different from that of the New Zealand which existed a mere 100 years ago.

earth, air, fire and water

Daybreak, still, cool, peaceful. The forests ripple with birdsong until suddenly the earth trembles. The horizon glows, first a dull red, then crimson. Soon the whole sky seems alight, not from the sunrise but from the earth itself. Waves of white hot pumice sweep the land. The sky rains ash and pumice until the sun dims to a pale orange disc. The earth is on fire from horizon to horizon. The forests blaze. Giant trees which minutes before stood firmly rooted are thrown on their sides, their foliage afire. Again and again the land heaves, until everything is dead.

This happened in the South Pacific. It happened in New Zealand only 1,800 years ago as volcanic action incinerated hundreds of km of countryside. This was nothing new. For at least 10,000 years there had been widespread volcanism around Mount Egmont and on the Auckland Peninsula. The volcanoes on the high central plateau, which were formed during the last two million years were still active 15,000 years ago. At that time volcanic lahars or mud flows poured from Mount Ruapehu carrying huge boulders long distances in vast muddy floods. One large boulder has been found near the present town of Bulls.

The volcanoes still rumble, parts of the land still smoke and the forests have yet to reclaim all their land. In the thermal regions today we can see in miniature the forces which continue to move continents.

New Zealand is a small country barely 1,600 km long, sitting astride the wind belt of the forties. Nowhere is it more than 128 km from the sea and yet there are high mountains generating glaciers and alpine meadows and lowlands clothed in luxuriant rain forests. It is a surprising and beautiful land. There are no native mammals with the exception of two bat species. Land snails living here are related to species long extinct in other countries.

There are primitive frogs, land birds which cannot fly and a strange reptile, the tuatara, the sole survivor of a race related to the dinosaurs, which died at least 60 million years ago. Together with these ancient elements, the new arrivals create a unique combination of plants and animals.

The origins of New Zealand, 200 million years ago, lie in the breakup of a vast southern continent, Gondwanaland, embracing the present continents of Antarctica, South America, Africa, North America, and Europe. New Zealand did not exist as a separate land mass for a further 65 million years when the first mountain building started and many of the ancient plants and animals arrived. The country was then much bigger than it is now.

There are fossil records of plants like kauri, lycopodium and podocarps in Jurassic rocks formed between 195-136 million years ago. There is additional fossil evidence of ferns, beech trees, New Zealand honeysuckle — *Knightia*, and *Dacrydium* in Cretaceous rocks which are between 136-65 million years old. Still further fossils involving Antarctic elements occur in early-mid Tertiary rocks which were formed about 30 million years ago. These include the genus *Phyllocladus* a member of which is the celery pine, *Astelia* a genus common throughout the country today, coprosmas with many present day species, *Fuchsia*, *Laurelia* and *Libocedrus*, best known as mountain cedar. Plants with tropical origins such as the rata, pandanus family, cabbage trees, mistletoes, and kamahi show up as fossils before the end of the Miocene period approximately eight million years ago. This establishes beyond doubt contact with other land masses.

The Tasman Sea began to form early enough to prevent land dinosaurs, snakes and marsupials from reaching the new land although links with the southern

Ngauruhoe
Near the site of the huge Taupo ash shower, Ngauruhoe is the most continously active of New Zealand volcanoes of recent times. The early Maoris witnessed many eruptions. The young cone of Ngauruhoe which has grown up on an old crater of Mount Tongariro now towers more than 328m higher than the older mountain and reaches a height of 2286m. The volcanoes are all situated in Tongariro National Park at the southern end of a zone of faulting,volcanism and thermal activity stretching for 1,600km across the South West Pacific.

8

continent of Gondwanaland continued long enough for some plants and animals to become widespread in other Southern Hemisphere countries including South America and South Africa.

Over millions of years the earth contorted, the climate changed, mountains were eroded almost to sea level and a new mountain building era began. These changes, caused by continental land movements, help to explain fossil coconuts on the northern peninsula, the absence of mammals and why New Zealand, which appears so isolated, should support plants and animals related to those of distant lands. The high level of endemism evident in so many native plants demonstrates that New Zealand has been separated from other land masses for millions of years.

In the last two million years large areas of New Zealand have been ice covered. The ice has expanded and contracted several times. Between each advance the climate was either similar to the present or sometimes warmer. In the warmer periods forest flourished while during the colder periods, when the ice advanced, the forests retreated and the sub-alpine grasslands expanded.

Water — the basis of life

Fumaroles — Waiotapu

Volcanic and thermal activity began at Waiotapu about 300,000 years ago when the area was covered by lake beds. There was a period of intense hydrothermal activity which resulted in water rising along faults from deep in the earth and the creation of a shallow reservoir of water below the old lakebed level. It was probably around 100,000 years ago that the area became eroded and the present cycle of activity commenced. Waiotapu covers 11.2 square km.

At the peak of the last ice age only 50,000 years ago, sub-alpine grassland covered Wellington, Wairarapa, Manawatu, Taranaki and Hawkes Bay. The Fiordland glaciers, often 2,000-3,000m deep extended to the sea where they formed an ice shelf as in Antarctica today. The sea level was 106m below its present level, Cook Strait was bridged and ice bergs were common off the New Zealand coast. Woody plants grew only in the North (Source —C. A. Fleming).

It is estimated that the West Coast glaciers still extended to the sea 13,400 years ago and that some time in the last 20,000 years the giant eagles, rails and flightless swans became extinct. The large flightless moas lingered on until about 1700AD although a few bush moas may have survived until the 1850s.

Because of these factors the land with its plants and animals has been changing ever since its creation. Species have become extinct, some have became localised while others have flourished over wide areas.

When Polynesian man first arrived, the land with its mountains, fiords, glaciers, volcanoes and deep forests had been formed. In pre-European times podocarp-hardwood forests covered large areas of the North Island, part of Westland, Banks Peninsula, Stewart Island and parts of Southland. Beech and beech-podocarp forest was confined, in the main, to the higher regions of the North Island, the north west of the South Island and Fiordland. Scrub or fernland clothed much of the central North Island extending to Hawkes Bay and Wairarapa. Lowland tussock flourished on the volcanic plateau and the east of the South Island while sub-alpine grasslands were confined to higher altitudes. Even this picture of pre-European vegetation neglects to mention the effects of Polynesian man who burned large areas of forest which was replaced by grass or scrubland.

Hells Gate, Rotorua

Glaciated Mountains

Not only does the weight of glacier ice erode, but the stones and rocks collected as it moves function in much the same way as sandpaper, scouring the rock and at times grinding it to a fine dust. In this way the land over which a glacier moves is stripped to bedrock and smoothed by its progress.

Lake Wakatipu

Snow fell in the mountains, collected on snowfields and compacted into glaciers that scoured some parts of the land for thousands of years. Where two glaciers merged, the ice mass was forced to move faster resulting in a deepening of the valley owing to increased erosion. Many New Zealand lakes occupy such deep trenches.

Algae in a water filled crater

Algae on Silica Terrace

Some species of alga are able to live at very high temperatures in thermal waters. The blue-green algae Cyanophyta are considered to be ancient plants and among the first to inhabit the earth in conditions similar to thermal regions today. The maximum temperatures which these algae seem to be able to withstand are 65-67°C.

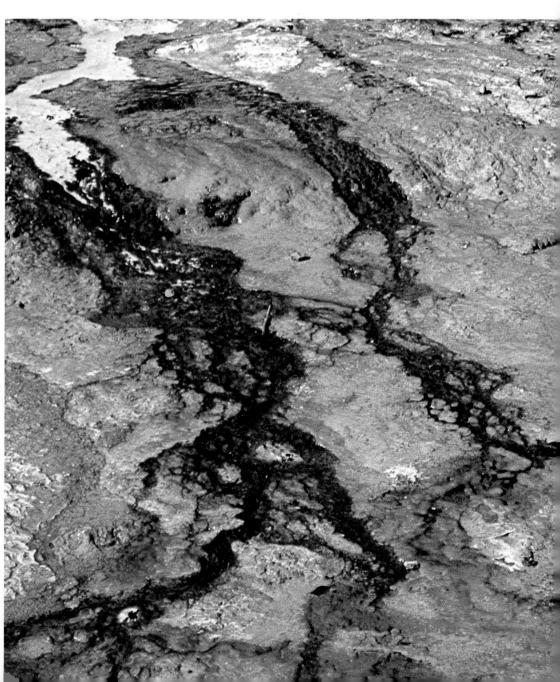

The First Plants
Amongst the first plants to colonize the land were lichens. They were able to grow on bare rock from sea level, where they were frequently doused by salt spray, to mountain chains where they were covered by snow and ice for months of the year. There are three main types of lichen, broadly described as crustose *(crust-like),* foliose *(leaflike) and* fruticose *(shrub-like).*

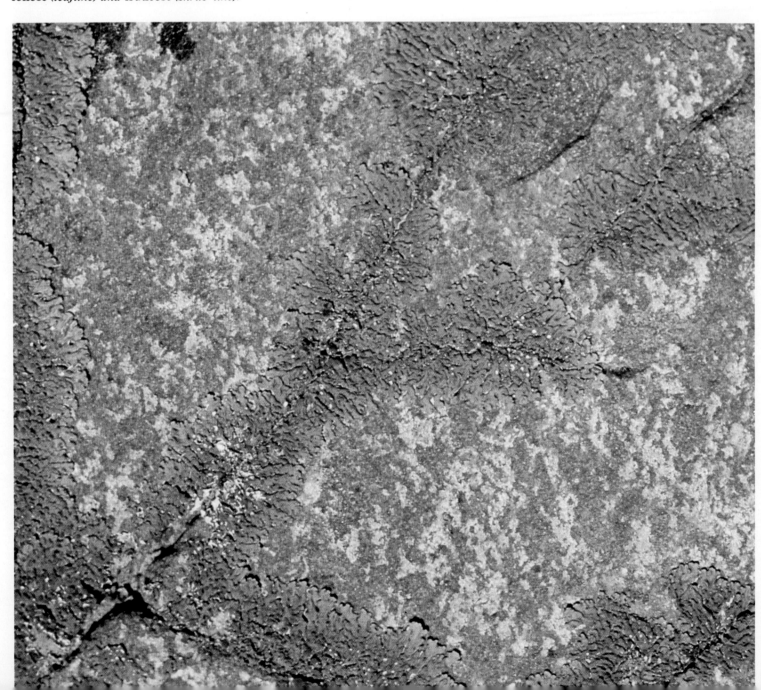

White Faced Heron — *Ardea novaehollandiae*
Up until 1940 this heron was a regular straggler from Australia. Now the most common heron in New Zealand, inhabiting coastal and inland areas, it is also native to the East Indies and New Guinea. Flocks of 20 or more are now quite often seen and although they usually nest singly their increasing numbers result in loose breeding colonies. The flimsy nests built in high trees usually contain a clutch of 3-5 pale blue/green eggs which take about 25 days to hatch. This heron is a graceful but strong flyer capable of gaining height quickly. Although normally silent they can utter a gutteral graa-aw.

Sandblast and surf

Contrasting with the gentle water communities of the swamps are the sand dunes in which all the plants and animals exist only under very different conditions. Here in the full blast of sea winds, there is no accumulation of mud, and violent wave action precludes both mangrove and glasswort. Originally there were about 121,460 hectares of dune country and in some places the coastal dunes were up to 9km wide. The community developed without the influence of browsing animals, but introduced plants and animals have altered both the appearance of the dunes and the importance of native plants in the sand-binding process.

Originally the dune cover was similar throughout the country although some plants such as spinifex do not grow in the southern regions. Regardless of location however, all dune plants that live on drifting sand are capable of binding it into a firm mass necessary for their survival.

In contrast to the sticky mud and tidal water of salt swamps the dunes are dry, continuously moving sand which in midsummer reach scorching temperatures. Yet plants which live here, cannot live elsewhere. Not far below the surface of any dune the sand is moist and it is this above all which enables the dune plants to grow. Even so plants must withstand an unstable surface and constant change. The foredunes facing the open sea are of course the most exposed and unstable and it is here that dunes form and reform from one season to the next. It is here also that the best known sand binder pingao is found. It is completely adapted for dune life with a leaf surface that can withstand the most severe sandblastings. The plant grows fast and can therefore escape burying. The tender growing points are protected and the plant is shaped to minimise wind resistance. Finally the wide network of its roots helps to secure the dune.

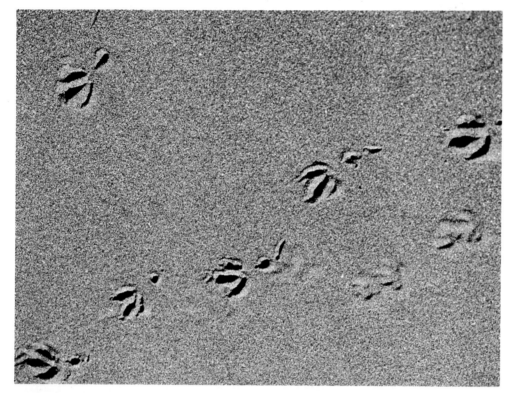

Bird tracks in the sand
The intertidal zone is an important foraging ground for all shore birds. Sandy coasts are frequented by oystercatchers, dotterels, the ever present gulls and often by the pipit which at the other end of its range can be seen feeding on the snow in alpine regions. In the sand dunes back from the beach, many of the shore birds nest, either singly like the dotterels or in colonies like the gulls. Each new tide brings new foraging opportunities.

Wind ripples in the sand

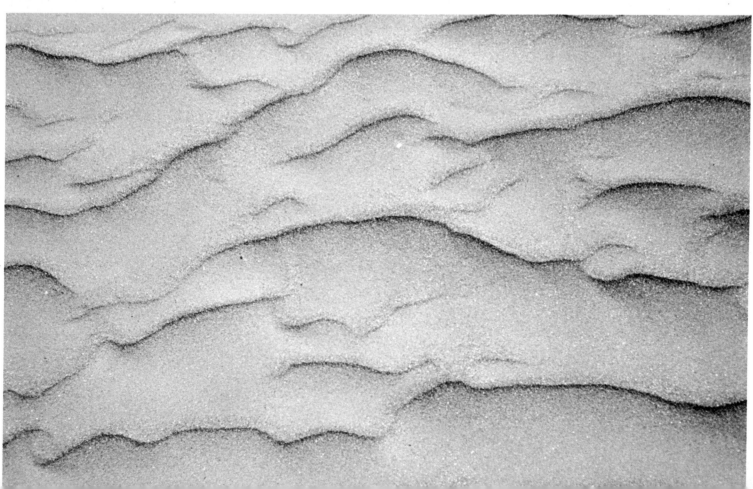

Pingao —*Desmoschoenus spiralis*
Growing solely in New Zealand, pingao is often the only plant which can withstand the full blast of sea winds. The foredunes take on a bronze hue, owing to the wiry foliage. Deep under the sand its rhizomes tap moisture that maintains the rest of the plant and enables it to keep sending out new shoots; this continual growth keeps the plant ahead of moving sand before it becomes buried. Flower heads and fruits can be seen in spring on sand dunes throughout the North, South and Stewart Islands.

The foredunes
The sand fixing ability of pingao on foredunes is well illustrated here where strong sea winds and tidal action are common. Less resilient dune plants such as sand convolvulus and coprosma cannot cope with the shifting sand and can only exist in the relative shelter of less exposed dunes.

Another dune plant, spinifex, is very common on many beaches. The sight of spinifex seed heads cartwheeling down a beach is common enough. Rain however will cause the sodden heads to collapse and gradually wind blown sand piles around the seed which germinates. If conditions are suitable the plant grows, more sand accumulates and in the plant's effort to keep ahead of the sand, a dune is formed. Behind the foredunes where the sand is more stable, grow the dainty shore convolvulus, sand coprosma, muehlenbeckia, sand pimelia and tauhinu.

The dunes may, in fact, create a whole complex of places where plants can grow including hollows, swamps and even shallow lakes. It depends on the stability of surrounding dunes, how long they last because wandering dunes can engulf them. The plants surrounding these ponds can grow prolifically and provide cover for water birds. On more barren pond sites, waders are constant visitors.

The more stable the dunes, the greater is the variety of plant life, although bare dunes do not support much animal life. In summer however, various wading birds such as dotterels are conspicuous. They scoop shallow nests in the sand and perform the decoying tactics, so familiar to many readers, in an attempt to lure intruders away from eggs and young.

On fixed dunes a stable clothing of vegetation permits shrubs and some trees to grow allowing forest birds to invade when fruits are ripening. It is not unusual to see bellbirds and tuis within a stone's throw of the beach. Dunes that have been fixed for a long time can support heavy stands of kohekohe, pohutukawa, ngaio or rata, but the locality determines which of these trees dominates. By this stage the dune cover has become coastal forest.

Gravel banks and rocky shores

Because rocky shores are more stable than the dunes, a greater variety of life abounds and a more complex community results. Spinifex and pingao can still be found but they are less important. The shore convolvulus too grows on the gravel banks but it is joined by plants which cannot live in sand. All of these plants live beyond the tidal range often amongst driftwood which has been stranded during severe storms. Silvery grey mats of raoulia or scabweed root in the gravel between low stands of rush. Brightly coloured lichens daub small rocks and as we move further up the beach coprosmas and the sprawling muehlenbeckia form rounded bushes.

Seabirds are conspicious even on exposed coasts. Oystercatchers and dotterels run along the banks, shags roost on the rocks, gulls scavenge and pipits forage in the seaweed. Many insects and spiders can live on these coasts. Under driftwood, earwigs, beetles, cockroaches, silverfish, katipo spiders and centipedes are found. The pacific gecko shelters by day under rocks and driftwood while the common skink suns itself by day and retires at night.

In spring and summer, moths, flies and small orange butterflies visit the flowers of the raoulia mats, the tiny green flowers of the coprosmas and the dainty white blossoms of the pimelia. Higher up the beach grow New Zealand flax, and larger plants which need more shelter.

Rocky headlands provide even greater opportunities for plants. On the Cook Strait coast, the ice plant, spaniard, mountain flax, woolyheads, pohuehue, koromiko, clematis, and several species of fern amongst many other plants crowd the rocks. Plants like taupata, koromiko, tauhinu and mountain flax attract nectar or fruit seeking birds such as the silvereye and bellbird. Again depending on location different types of plants can dominate. On northern cliffs pohutukawa is common.

Spinifex — *Spinifex hirsutus*
Sometimes known as tumbleweed, this plant too is well adapted to sand dune life for it can stand sandblast, moving sand and occasional burying. Its distribution is not as wide as pingao as it is not found in the southern part of the South Island. The seed heads shown here are a common sight cartwheeling down a sandy beach.

Elsewhere flax, ngaio, hebes or in the south olearia and senecio are conspicuous.

On many headlands birds, either singly or in colonies, nest during the summer months. Terns, reef herons, shags and gulls all frequent the coast and are seen by day while the small blue penguins waddle ashore at night to occupy their burrows. Black backed gull colonies covering several hectares are found in many areas. The adult gulls make nests of seaweed and grass on the gravel banks and lay two or three speckled eggs. The downy chicks hatch twenty-nine days later and are common during December. Anyone who has been in a gull colony knows the resulting commotion. First, the gulls which seem to constantly circle the colony call a warning. The others, by then alerted, stay with their eggs and young as long as possible then launch into a wheeling, screaming flock that divebomb the intruder until he retreats. The same treatment is given to any other large birds or animals that pose a threat. Once the intruder is repulsed the adults quickly return to shelter the eggs or chicks and the colony returns to relative calm.

The forests begin

Progressing inland from dunes, swamps or rocky shores brings us to the taller trees. In many areas there is coastal scrub but since scrub acts as a nursery for larger plants, it is usually a temporary community indicating a progression to coastal forest. Very few of the strictly coastal trees can tolerate more than a few degrees of frost and nearly all belong to families which have representatives in the tropics. It is not surprising therefore that most are confined to the warmer coastal areas of the North Island especially the Auckland district.

Characteristically, the canopy is flattened due to wind, trees grow close together and are much lower than the trees of the inland forests. Many normal podocarp hardwood forest plants are found in coastal forests and in some place the forest which extends almost to the water's edge is merely normal podocarp-hardwood forest protected only by a narrow strip of more salt tolerant trees. No distinct dividing line exists and the forest types merge one with the other until the frost tender plants are eliminated.

30

Horokaka, Maori Ice Plant — *Disphyma australe*
This native ice plant, not to be confused with the larger introduced plant, has flowers only 2.5cm in diameter. It is a native of cliff faces and rocky outcrops in coastal regions on all main islands and some of the smaller off shore islands as well. Like all succulents it stores water in the fleshy leaves to help it through the long spells when it is without fresh water.

Shore Convolvulus — *Calystegia soldanella*
Like the other native species of convolvulus the little shore convolvulus is not endemic. It grows in coastal areas in North, South, Stewart, Chatham and Kermadec Islands, as well as on the shores of some inland lakes. Flowers occur between October/March.

Yellow Sand Coprosma — *Coprosma acerosa*

Approximately 90 species of coprosmas are known throughout the world and all but one of the 45 species in New Zealand is endemic. The name meaning 'smell of dung' results from two early discovered species which have an unpleasant smell. They belong to the family Rubiaceae *which includes plants like* Coffea *and* Cinchona *which yield coffee and quinine respectively. All the New Zealand species are woody but range from creeping mats to small trees and occur in almost all situations from the coast to sub-alpine scrub and fell field. The sand coprosma, found on the North, South, Stewart and Chatham Islands generally grows in the shelter of dune hollows and forms a tight low growing shrub, thus becoming a good sand catcher. This photograph shows a piece removed from bush to illustrate the branching habit. The leaves are small and rolled to reduce water loss during the hot summer months.*

31

Cape Kidnappers
These cliffs, near Cape Kidnappers, the site of New Zealand's only mainland gannet colony, contain marine deposits of the Pliocene-Pleistocene *period (2-7 million years ago) and layers of ash from Central North Island volcanic eruptions.*

Katipo Spider — *Latrodectus katipo*, one of New Zealand's poisonous spiders, is seldom found more than 30m from the sea. Only the female is capable of biting and then only when an adult. The adult male is much smaller than the female which when mature has an abdomen about the size of a garden pea. She is black and shiny as illustrated and frequently misidentified. Katipos are most commonly found on sandy beaches and their tangled webs are always spun close to the ground either at the base of grasses or sedges or under driftwood. They can be found along most of the North Island Coast and in the South Island as far south as Dunedin in the east, and fairly well down the West Coast.

Beetles which comprise most of the katipos food are caught and hauled well above the ground until the spider is ready to eat. At that time digestive juices are forced through a small hole from which the spider sucks the digested body material. When feeding is complete the insect has become an empty shell.

The katipo belongs to a widespread genus *Latrodectus* which includes the black widow spider of North America. The effects of a bite in humans is often severe, the poison particularly effecting the nervous system. Victims usually recover however, after a few days.

Pohuehue — *Muehlenbeckia complexa* Tight, springy and tangled masses of pohuehue are a feature of many coasts. Although most obvious on coastal areas it grows also in lowland and lower montane forests. There are seven named forms of this species in the New Zealand Flora.

Black Stink Roach — *Platyzosteria novaeseelandiae* Although not confined to coastal regions the stink roach is commonly found during daylight hours under driftwood. At night this native cockroach emerges to feed on decaying vegetable and animal matter. It is common to find a number together. When disturbed they run quickly, constantly moving their sensitive antennae as they move. They are capable of leaving a heavy and unpleasant odour which has earned the name stink roach.

Australian Gannet — *Sula bassana serrator*

An estimated life span of 25-29 years makes the gannet one of the longest living seabirds. Adult birds range widely throughout our seas in summer and winter although juvenile birds migrate to the coastal waters off Australia during the colder months. With the exception of Cape Kidnappers, all breeding colonies occur on offshore islands either off New Zealand or Tasmanian and south-east Australian coasts. Small surface fish are caught by gannets plunging from the air into the sea. The bird has no external nostrils and is well adapted to withstand the sudden impact.

In the southern fiords, beech forest grows almost to the water's edge along with some sub-alpine plants. On the exposed coasts of Stewart Island a sub-alpine scrub of leatherwood grows to sea level reflecting the severity of the climate. Only one coastal tree the rata *Metrosideros umbellata,* can claim to be a true coastal tree of the south although ngaio does grow as far south as Dunedin, although it is rare at that latitude.

For the true coastal trees we return to the north. The most famous one is the pohutukawa, the magnificent member of the rata family which in recent times has been cultivated well south of its normal range. On the shores of East Cape, Northland and the Hauraki Gulf it once covered large areas. Most of it has gone. Pohutukawa forest has an undergrowth generally more open than normal rain forest but still supporting many species. Tree ferns, lianes, kawakawa, karo, five finger, astelias, and masses of kiekie are all found in the forest. So too are small ferns and mosses although again they cannot compete in variety or luxuriance with the damp podocarp forests further inland.

Another beautiful tree confined to the north is the puriri. Although once widespread it did not form communities which could be called puriri forests. Today owing to European settlers felling the trees for their hard wood, much of it has gone. The karaka with its large shiny leaves is another coastal tree that seems to withs-

tand salt blasts much more readily than others. It generally grows in groves and often in association with other plants like kiekie, ngaio, whauo (cork tree) and manuka. The interior of the forest is often open with a litter of dry leaves and berries in various stages of decay.

The ngaio forest occurs widely, its composition depending largely on the amount of salt spray. In some very exposed areas the trees are dwarfed by wind causing the branches to spread sideways rather than upwards. Plants normally found within ngaio forest include taupata, kawakawa and poroporo but as always the actual locality decides the species likely to be present.

There is a further tree kohekohe which in association with other trees has been described by some authors as a semi-coastal plant. It occurs in forests which are ecologically similar to lowland forest but which will withstand only light frosts and little salt. These forests are best developed in the North Island and the northern part of the South Island. Kawakawa is very common in the understory, along with kiekie, coprosmas, ngaio and various ferns. Again because so much of the forests occupy land suitable for farming only small remnants remain. In all of these forests, the normal forest birds are found and in early summer when the plants are flowering the fragrant air vibrates with the low hum of insects in their millions.

Milford Sound-Fiordland
In the southern fiords which are protected from the salt blast of the open sea beech forest grows almost to the high tide level. Originally scoured out by glaciers descending to the ocean, these long U-shaped valleys, now flooded by the sea, create unique environments. The deepest part of Milford sound is over 500m and the top of Mitre Peak is said to be the highest point of any mountain in the world which rises sheer out of the sea. So steep are the valley sides and so hard is the base rock that the forest cannot build up much humus before the weight of the trees, aided no doubt by the high rainfall cause landslides which send long ribbons of forest crashing into the sea. Scars showing various stages of regeneration are common throughout the area.

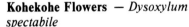

Kohekohe Flowers — *Dysoxylum spectabile*

Known to early European settlers as New Zealand cedar, kohekohe is actually the region's only member of the mahogany family. It is unique amongst native trees for being cauliflorous; that is the flowers grow out of the trunk and main branches not on the outer twigs. The mahogany family of 800 species is normally confined to tropical rain forests but kohekohe grows in coastal and lowland forests, sometimes being the dominant tree. It is restricted to the North Island and the northern part of the South Island, where mature trees may grow 15 m tall. Once an abundant tree, it has suffered badly from animal damage and land clearance.

Karo — *Pittosporum crassifolium*

Karo occurs naturally only in the Auckland Province and on Kermadec Islands although it is now naturalised further south. It grows on forest margins and stream sides, often in association with pohutukawa. The sweetly scented flowers develop into green seed capsules which when ripe split into three equal parts exposing shiny black and sticky seeds. There are about 26 endemic species described in the New Zealand Flora *and there appear to be many wild and cultivated hybrids. There is also evidence of natural hybridisation. The pittosporum family of over 200 species is widespread but mainly of tropical or sub-tropical distribution.*

37

Red Billed Gull — *Larus novaehollandiae scopulinus*

Confined to the New Zealand region including some off shore islands this pretty little gull is closely related to the black billed gull also found around our coasts, and the silver gull of the Australian waters. There is some difference in the New Zealand populations, the sub-antarctic race having shorter, stouter bills and slightly darker plumage. Their food consists of small fish, any animal matter they can scavenge and when inland, worms. They also behave as robber gulls, forcing other sea birds to give up food. It is estimated that there are breeding colonies in about 160 widely scattered localities most of which are in coastal areas and about 40,000 breeding pairs. These colonies nearly all of which are on lee shores range from 12 pairs to many thousands. White fronted terns are frequently found breeding in association with them.

38

Karaka — *Corynocarpus laevigatus*
Karaka is a true coastal tree although confined to the warmer coasts of North, South, Kermadec and Chatham Islands. Because the seeds germinate so easily karakas commonly occur in groves where the canopy may be up to 15 metres high. As with taupata the flowers are small and insignificant but the fruits which ripen in April are better known. Karaka was one of the few indigenous plants grown by the early Maoris and this may account for part of its present distribution. The kernel of its orange fruit was part of the Maori's staple diet. These berries unless treated correctly are poisonous causing permanent deformities or death in humans. Karaka is endemic but belongs to a genus with only a few species which are found in the New Hebrides, Queensland, and New Caledonia.

Pacific Gecko — *Hoplodactylus pacificus*
This gecko is found under driftwood in coastal areas and in forests all over New Zealand. There is great pattern and colour variation between individuals although unlike the forest gecko it cannot change its colour to any great extent. The geckos mature when about four years old, live in the wild for at least ten years and have been kept in captivity for twenty years. When fully grown they measure up to 15 cm long. They emerge at night to feed, not only on insects and spiders, but on a wide variety of fleshy fruits and berries as well as nectar and some fleshy leaves. Skins are shed 3-4 times during the summer when they are most active but not at all in the winter months. Geckos usually shed their skins in one piece. The skin splits first near the head then peels back off the body.

Taupata — *Coprosma repens*
Best known as taupata, this coastal coprosma occurs naturally from North Cape to Marlborough on rocky shores. The shiny bright green leaves and bright orange berries are more attractive than the green insignificant flowers. The male and the female flowers occur on separate plants. As the plant is wind pollinated large amounts of pollen are produced. Taupata, like many New Zealand plants, is very adaptable. When in a sheltered situation it grows as a small tree but when exposed to fierce winds it adopts a prostrate form.

New Zealand Flax — *Phormium tenax*
Totally unrelated to the European flax, New Zealand flax is a large perennial monocotyledon. Found throughout New Zealand including Stewart and Chatham Islands it also occurs on Norfolk Island. It grows in coastal and lowland areas thriving in places which are periodically flooded or close to running water. The plant remains relatively small when growing in stagnant water. The leaves, which are often 2m long, are very strong with a cell and fibre structure that keeps the leaves erect. The flowers are supported on a stalk up to 4 m high and in season attract nectar-feeding birds. Today garden *varieties are cultivated, not for the fibre as formerly, but for their attractive foliage.*

Cabbage Tree — *Cordyline australis*
What has become known as the cabbage tree is neither a cabbage nor a tree but like the New Zealand flaxes -phormium sp, *now placed in the family* Agavaceae. *It is the most widespread of the five species confined to New Zealand. It occurs on North, South, and Stewart Islands in open places, forest margins, and near swamps up to about 800 metres. In summer the flowers produce a sweet scent which attracts insects in hundreds.*

Pohutukawa — *Metrosideros excelsa*
Now introduced to other parts of New Zealand, pohutukawa grows naturally around the coast of Auckland, Coromandel Peninsula, and the Bay of Plenty. It is closely related to the forest ratas and like the largest of them grows up to 21m high. The trunk however is short and the developing branches become crooked, spreading and massive. The flowers occur about Christmas and by the time flowering is over have turned the surrounding ground to a dull red with their stamens. There are some 20 species of Metrosideros *throughout Australia, New Zealand, Malaysia, and Polynesia, 10 being confined to New Zealand. A similar tree* Metrosideros umbellata *is characteristic of southern regions although unlike the pohutukawa is not confined to the coastal areas. It grows as a shrub or tree 12-18m high and occurs in some sub-antarctic islands as well as the South Island.*

Keikei — *Freycinetia banksii*
Refer page 71

Common Skink — *Leiolopisma zelandica*
The common skink although often seen in coastal areas, also occurs in many open areas such as river beds, cultivated gardens and even tussock mountain tops up to 1700m. They are mostly seen basking in the sun or scuttling to safety. Their distribution is confined to the South Island and the lower half of the North Island. North of Taupo they are replaced by another species. They eat insects and the fruits of native plants, measure approximately 15 cm when fully grown and give birth to up to ten young at a time.

42

the gentle earth

It is quiet, still and dark; we are surrounded by dense vegetation. My friends from Europe are struck dumb by the confusion of plants. They had not expected a forest like this in the temperate zone of the South Pacific. Finally one of them moves to the base of a huge miro, its trunk rising out of sight, and touches it. He turns: "It is so beautiful, so wild — I have not been in jungle before."

We were in a podocarp-hardwood forest on the lower slopes of Mount Ruapehu. Ahead was a cluster of tree ferns, to our right a tangle of lianes, to our left a screen of twiggy undergrowth. Overhead the trees met to form a canopy, while underfoot a carpet of moss and fern cushioned our footsteps.

A podocarp is a member the plant family *Podocarpaceae*, the smallest of which grows only in alpine regions and reaches a maximum height of about 30cm and the largest of which are tall trees such as totara, miro, matai, rimu and kahikatea. Where any one of these trees dominates a locality the forest often takes on its name; hence totara forest, rimu forest and so on. The hardwoods are smaller trees like tawa and kamahi which generally form the canopy.

Before the fires of Polynesian man the forest covered large areas of New Zealand, particularly the North Island. In Pre-European times it spread from the great kauri forests of the far north down both coasts, skirting in the main the

volcanoes of the central plateau, and thrust on to the present-day barrier of Cook Strait. In the South Island the forest covered a large portion of the West Coast, occurred on the east at Banks Peninsula and Kaikoura and finally as a coastal strip on the south east facing Stewart Island. The forest increased in complexity and luxuriance the further north it grew.

Remnants of the forest are located in the Waipoua State Forest of the northern peninsula, Mount Egmont National Park, West Coast of the South Island and Stewart Island with numerous smaller concentrations on the foothills of most ranges.

Similarities to tropical forests

Strangers may be excused for calling podocarp-hardwood forests "jungle" because they are true rain forest. They require a minimum of 75cm rain spread evenly throughout the year. Several months drought can in fact destroy much forest, although excess rainfall does no harm. In some parts of Fiordland, for

instance, between 625 and 750cm fall each year. Elsewhere 150 to 200cm is not unusual.

The trees and shrubs with one or two exceptions are evergreen. Large trees are often supported by buttressed roots, while the roots of many plants stretch horizontally across the floor. Colonies of tree ferns are numerous; small ferns occur in profusion. Decomposing logs and vegetation litter the forest floor, which is carpeted with moss, liverwort, lichen and filmy fern. Lianes create tangles which when combined with dense undergrowth make human progress extremely slow. This is especially true of gullies.

The forest grows in several levels. At the top, emerging through the canopy are the tallest podocarps — rimu, miro, matai, totara, kahikatea and sometimes the huge northern rata — *Metrosideros robusta*. The canopy itself consists of shorter trees — tawa, kamahi, puketea, hinau and maire. These are often draped with flowering vines which have struggled up to the light. Small orchids also appear

Mount Ruapehu —*Podocarp Forest Interior*

Coromandel Forest Park

The forest here appears more tropical than the podocarp-hardwood forest counterpart farther south. There are more species and a greater general abundance of plants. This locality is an ideal plant growing environment with a high rainfall as well as mild winters. There is evidence that plants are at least keeping ahead of browsing animals. The plants shown here include, nikau, five finger, supplejack, kiekie, and tree ferns, all of which have tropical affinities.

in the upper storey of the canopy although they are also found at lower levels. A third level comprises tree ferns, small trees and large shrubs including toru, lemonwood, tawari, mahoe, lancewood, fivefinger, nikau palms, cabbage trees and lacebarks. Below this are the shrubby plants such as coprosmas, kawakawa, horopito, karapapa and mairehau. Finally the ground is covered with ferns, ground orchids, nettles and sprawling lycopodium.

A piece of tramping advice is: "When you get lost or want a good view ahead, climb a tree". Good advice — but first find a tree that you can climb. The mature podocarps, because they rise unbranched for so many metres, are out of the question, so you've got to make do with the canopy trees. Even these can be difficult to scale and if you succeed, you gain little more than a view of other tree tops unless the forest is growing on a reasonable slope.

Bats the only mammals

In pre-human times bats were the only land mammals in New Zealand. One, the short-tailed bat, is peculiar to this country while the long-tailed bat is found in Australia as well. Both are now rare. It is the absence of mammals which makes the forest so different from its rain forest counterparts in other countries. The only conspicuous native animals are birds and insects. Now, however, the mammals introduced by Europeans have initiated vast changes. Deer and goats browse the lower plants, pigs root the forest floor, possums attack the canopy and rats eat seeds and fruit.

Fight for light

Within this delicately adjusted plant community exists the eternal struggle for a place to live. To say that all plants strive to reach the sun is however to oversimplify. Those plants which demand light reach for the forest margin or canopy but there are many plants which

Fungi

Fungi include moulds, mildews, and toadstools. They are primarily decomposers, helping bacteria to break down dead organisms, and thus recycling plant and animal tissue. Unlike flowering plants they contain no chlorophyl and therefore do not require sunlight to manufacture food. They have no roots like higher plants but are composed of minute and delicate hyphae which exude powerful digestive juices. The juices penetrate and soften the matter in which the fungus grows and make it ready for absorption by the plant. To reproduce, fungi produce millions of spores. A single field mushroom for instance releases 16,000 million spores in its short life while a woody bracket fungus may over a six month growing period release 30 billion spores a day. The spores are microscopic and the vast numbers are produced to overcome problems of dispersal. (Source — Marie Taylor, see bibliography.)

47

(c)

(d)

(e)

(f)

Podocarps

Rimu — Dacrydium cupressinum (a)
Totara — Podocarpus totara (b)
Kahikatea — Podocarpus dacrydioides (c)
Tanekaha — Phyllocladus trichomanoides (d)
Miro — Podocarpus Ferrugineus (e)
Hall's totara — Podocarpus hallii (f)

Within the podocarp family are some seven genera and over 100 species most of them confined to the Southern Hemisphere. The four New Zealand genera are represented in these photos by *totara*-Podocarpus totara, *rimu*-Dacrydium cupressinum, *tanekaha*-Phyllocladus trichomanoides and *kahikatea*-Podocarpus dacrydioides. We have eight endemic species of podocarpus, *three* dacrydium, *and three* of phyllocladus, *although by no means all of them are found in podocarp-hardwood forests. Podocarps are types of conifers and bear male and female 'cones' or spikes rather than flowers. In all species male and female cones appear on different trees.*

Alseuosmia sp

This genus, endemic to New Zealand, displays a great variety of leaf form and possibly hybridism. This specimen photographed in the Tauherenikau Valley — Tararua Ranges was one of many growing in sheltered but open areas on the valley floor. I have also photographed a similar plant in the podocarp-hardwood forest on Mount Ruapehu.

Lichens

The forest in general lacks areas of conspicuous colour, a casual look revealing little but foliage green. We have to look instead to small objects like this lichen, less than 1 cm in diameter, for colour. There are over 1000 species of lichens which occur naturally in New Zealand. Many of these also grow naturally in Tasmania, Australia, South America and the Northern Hemisphere. New Zealand has been described as the botanical headquarters of several large and conspicuous lichen genera. There are few common names and those which do exist are often confused with mosses This photograph shows a crustose lichen growth on an alga covered stone.

Kahikatea — *Podocarpus dacrydioides*
Kahikatea, the tallest of native trees reaching 60m tall, once formed extensive forests. Formerly more plentiful in areas such as the swamps of the Hauraki Plains, the largest surviving areas are now in South Westland. Stands which may take up to 800 years to mature were cleared off many lowland areas for farming and the soft white odourless wood used for cases in which butter was exported.
The juvenile leaves are arranged in 2 rows either side of a twig, while the adult leaves are overlapping and closely pressed to the twig. Male catkin-like cones and female 'flowers' occur on different trees. A mature tree can produce about four and a half million seeds in a good year according to A. E. Beveridge, attracting tuis, pigeons and bellbirds, which assist seed disposal. Kahikatea grows from North Cape to Bluff, on most fertile lowlands and can tolerate frequent flooding.

Giant Moss — *Dawsonia superba*
What appear to some people as pine seedlings are in fact large mosses. They occur in damp forests such as the Tararua Range and Mount Egmont National Park.

Native Frog —*Leiopelma archeyi*
All three native frogs are rare, protected and possess a number of primitive features. They have for instance two tail wagging muscles but no tails, no ear drums and no eustachian tubes or vocal sacs. The only noise which they can produce is a high pitched squeak. At the same time they possess some well advanced features such as large eyes and night vision which help them as they are nocturnal.

52

Montane Podocarp — Hardwood Forest Interior

One of the last patches of truly virgin forest is shown in this 140 degrees panorama. The elevation is approximately 800m, and we are in a montane forest where the wind shorn trees stand little more than 3m high. Their moss-covered trunks twist and intertwine. The forest floor, continually damp from rain and mist to the point of almost being boggy, supports a very heavy carpet of moss and lichen. In this locality there are no signs of introduced mammals so that the floor is untrampled and foliage flourishes as in pre-European times. A botanist looking at this photograph will immediately notice the prolific regeneration, especially the grass-like astelia and the five-finger — Pseudopanax discolor, plants that have been greatly reduced if not eliminated from most similar localities. Travel through this forest while botanically exciting is physically demanding as well. One continuously climbs, under and round, and is never able to walk in a straight line.

cannot tolerate direct sun and avoid bright light. The interior of thick forest is like a glasshouse. It is generally warmer, there is more moisture in the air and the temperature does not fluctuate as much as outside. This is borne out by trampers who prefer the night shelter of forest to scrub if they have a choice. In these sheltered conditions, ferns, mosses and lichens abound. Many of them are able to absorb moisture through the leaves, an adaptation to their surroundings where they receive little direct rain. When a large tree falls and creates a clearing we see the relatively quick growth of light-demanding shrubs. Once established they give protection to the seedlings of larger trees which eventually overtop the shrubs.

With their light cut off the shrubs die. Manuka is an important nursery plant in this respect. Today large areas are covered by manuka scrub following forest destruction and most New Zealanders know how difficult it is to penetrate.

The pattern of regeneration in Northland kauri forest, for instance, follows this pattern. Manuka scrub matures into manuka forest allowing kauri seedlings to establish in the nursery-like atmosphere. The kauris grow, overtop the manuka and deprive it of light. It dies. Taraire then grows and humus forms on the floor, allowing other plants to become established. This pattern typifies the slow but constant change in all New Zealand forests.

Puzzling plant barriers

There are two convenient, if blurred, latitudinal divisions marking plant distribution. One is at 38 degrees South running roughly from the Raukumara range, through the southern Kaimais and out to Kawhia Harbour. Some plants and animals are confined to the north of this line while a good many others either barely reach or overreach it. It is significant that, although even more blurred, this division applies to marine flora as well. Important plants confined to the north are kauri, toatoa, tawhero and makamaka. Likewise certain plants flourish or are found only south of the 38th parallel. The significance of this division is puzzling but probably the result of temperature change. It has been suggested also that it marks the northern boundary of the huge ash showers from the central volcanoes, which destroyed vast areas of vegetation. Whatever the cause, this division adds further interest because it has caused the development of related yet different species, thus increasing the floral variety.

The second broad latitudinal division occurs at 42 degrees South running from Tapuaenuku in the east of the South Island and out through the northern Paparoa range. This division is not as dramatic because fewer species are involved. Again some species are confined to the north or south or seldom seen on either side.

Evolution taking place

Many trees and shrubs are confined to this country while others are related to species in forests throughout South America, Tasmania, New Guinea and Australia. The coprosmas for instance reach their greatest degree of variation here. It is thought that they developed early in New Zealand's history, later becoming more widespread. To appreciate why an isolated and small land area supports such great plant variety we should remember that the plants have undergone a series of fairly rapid adjustments as the glaciers which once covered much of the country advanced and retreated. The forests either expanded or contracted as a result. Sometimes as segments were isolated from the remainder, new species evolved. Consider for instance that 13,400 years ago the glaciers of the West Coast extended to the sea. Today forest occupies much of the old glacial paths. In the North Island the volcanic ash shower 1800 years ago laid bare some 12,800 square km of land but when the Europeans arrived a century ago heavy forest blanketed the land from the central volcanoes to the west coast. The theory that many plants are still evolving is supported by the number of species which hybridise in the wild. Nurserymen, too, have realised this and recent years have seen an increase in the varieties of native plants cultivated.

Poroporo — *Solanum laciniatum*
One of the three New Zealand species belonging to the potato family, it grows in coastal and inland areas free from frost and where there is plenty of light. It belongs to a large, mostly tropical family which contains numerous narcotic or poisonous species. It is related to some edible plants such as tomato, cape gooseberry and eggplant but also to poisonous plants like deadly nightshade. It is reported that early colonists made jam from the fleshy orange berries which are widely spread by birds.

Broadleafed Cabbage Tree —*Cordyline indivisa*
Found in wetter mountains from Hunua and Coromandel Ranges to Fiordland, the broad leaves are probably an adaptation to a wetter environment. There are several other cabbage tree species with horticultural forms.

Supplejack Berries — *Ripogonum scandens*
This unusual member of the lily family is abundant throughout podocarp-hardwood forest. In lowland forests this endemic liane creates inpenetrable barriers. While the flowers are green and inconspicuous, the berries are bright red. Supplejack grows in the North, South, Stewart and Chatham Islands and the genus is distributed throughout New Guinea, Australia, New Zealand.

Toadstools — *Mycena sp.*
This group of fungi reappeared 2 years in a row on the same piece of earth during the damp and warm spring months. Each time they lasted barely 4 days before shrivelling away to nothing.

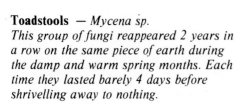

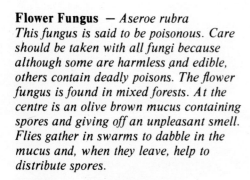

Flower Fungus — *Aseroe rubra*
This fungus is said to be poisonous. Care should be taken with all fungi because although some are harmless and edible, others contain deadly poisons. The flower fungus is found in mixed forests. At the centre is an olive brown mucus containing spores and giving off an unpleasant smell. Flies gather in swarms to dabble in the mucus and, when they leave, help to distribute spores.

Carabid — *Mecodema simplex*
Carabids are commonly found under logs and stones and it is very difficult to determine the species without dissection. Most carabids, both at beetle and larvae stage, are predators. The adults cannot fly because the wing covers are fused. They hunt at night, both the beetles and larvae attacking cicada nymphs.

Copper Skink — *Leiolopisma aeneum*
Confined to the North Island it inhabits damp sites in scrub or forest from which it seldom emerges to sun itself like other members of its family. It hunts in the litter of the forest floor for small invertebrates and when fully grown measures 15cms long. As with all skinks several young are born at a time. It is difficult for unskilled people to tell the sexes apart. Skinks, like geckos shed their skins but scale by scale rather than in one piece. When hunted or roughly handled both skinks and geckos cast off their tails. New tails grow to replace the old ones although the skin of the new tail is usually a slightly different colour and the pattern of the scales varies.

Huhu Grubs — *Prionoplus reticularis*
The huhu, the largest of New Zealand's long horn beetles, is nocturnal and capable of a powerful but nonpoisonous nip. It breeds in dead trees of every kind assisting decay. Long chambers are eaten out by the larvae. The adult female lays white cigar shaped eggs, in groups under bark or in crevices. The larvae which hatch within three weeks take 2-3 years to mature, and make their way closer to the bark to pupate. The adults begin emerging in November and continue through until February. They make a whirring noise in flight and land heavily. They are hunted by moreporks. In the 1800s the larvae were a favourite food of the now extinct huia.

57

Orange Fern Frond — *Blechnum capense*
The genus Blechnum *includes over 200 species most of which are found in the Southern Hemisphere. This species which has no common name, occurs throughout the New Zealand region including the sub-antarctic islands. It is found in many other countries including South Africa, South America, Australia, Pacific Islands, and Malaya. The fronds uncurl as they grow and the bright colour fades. (Left and facing page.)*

Kidney Fern — *Cardiomanes reniforme*
Both endemic and unique, the kidney fern is found in both podocarp-hardwood and beech forests where it can carpet the ground and lower trunks over large areas. It grows from sea level to about 900m and curls in dry weather, to conserve moisture. The sori which produce the spores are arranged around the margin.

Lake Waikaremoana (Sunset)

The forests surrounding Lake Waikaremoana form the 1,240 square km of Urewera National Park, one of the biggest parks in New Zealand. It has the largest remaining area of virgin forest and shows considerable variation from area to area within its boundaries. Lake Waikaremoana has a shore line of 200km and a depth of over 240m. Kakas, bush falcons, parakeets, pigeons and tuis are all seen in the area.

60

Ferns — *Blechnum discolor*

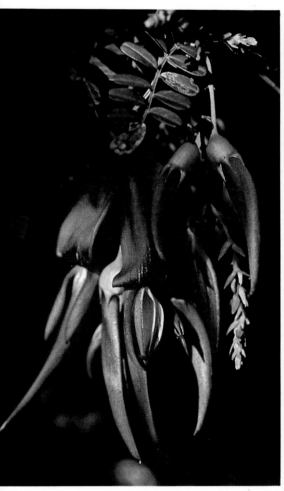

Kaka Beak — *Clianthus puniceus*
Now widely cultivated, it seems that the kaka beak has always been a rare plant in the wild. It is now uncommon on the mainland in its normal habitat. It was previously cultivated by Maoris and is now grown widely in gardens. Kaka beak is confined to the North Island, on inlets from the Bay of Islands to Tolaga Bay, and various places on the adjacent mainland.

Treeferns (Waikaremoana)
New Zealand has nine mainland species of treefern. The different species vary in distribution, some being confined to heavy lowland forest where a thick soil has accumulated. Treeferns reach their southern most limits in New Zealand.

Ferns, ferns, ferns

Ferns are found everywhere from dry exposed banks to the sheltered, constantly wet margins of waterfalls. The filmy ferns with few exceptions grow only where sufficient moisture prevents drying. They are most common in the forest interior where moss and fern can form a continuous carpet; some of the larger mosses mimicking the forms of small ferns. Many people are unaware of the shapes, patterns, colour and variety of the small plants growing in the glass house-type shelter. The unique kidney fern for example continues to surprise because of its 'unfern like' fronds. New Zealand has a very large fern flora, including nine mainland tree ferns, the silver fern being the best known.

Giant trees and tiny flowers

The insignificance of many flowers is almost a characteristic of the podocarp-hardwood forest. Of course there are exceptions such as clematis, rata vine, kamahi and rewarewa but many flowers are minute or found so high above the ground that they are seldom seen. Forest plants in other countries are much more showy and it is interesting to speculate why New Zealand forest flowers are generally so small. It is clear however that plants have reproduced successfully and occupied large land areas. In spite of the small blossoms the forest assumes a sweet smell in the early summer accompanied by the hum of insects which is absent in the winter months.

Subtlety of the seasons

To the casual observer the forest changes little with the seasons and for most, it is not an inviting place in mid-winter. The evergreen foliage and small flowers result in few dramatic changes. There are, however, many subtle changes. Spring emerges from the blanket of winter in September. Tiny flowers appear on the toru, rangiora blooms, clematis showers parts of the canopy, and certain small ground orchids emerge. There are still few insects and courting birds are not obvious. Although not comparable with the new growth of introduced plants, the forest develops a more yellow-green colour.

As summer approaches and the days lengthen, migrating cuckoos arrive and add a new sound to the forest. Insects, which through the winter months are virtually absent, begin to flourish. As summer develops the insect hum increases and reaches its climax with the emergence of cicadas from the ground, where they have been feeding on plant roots for at least 3 years. At their peak the noise is deafening although their numbers show marked differences some years.

The time to hunt for flowers is early summer because the long hot summer days soon turn them into dry seed heads. Filmy ferns curl to conserve water. Should a drought persist, leaves of many forest plants hang limply.

As the days begin to shorten in autumn, the still warm weather and rain showers encourage brief outbreaks of fungi, some brilliantly coloured. At the same time the heavily scented, almost overpowering, perching orchid — *Earina autumnalis,* breaks into flower, a sure sign that summer has slipped away. With the crispening of the temperature, the cuckoos depart and numerous berries colour the forest.

Often the berries are more striking than the flowers from which they developed. The berries in turn attract wood pigeons, tuis, silvereyes and other birds.

Winter merges with autumn, the days close in, rain becomes frequent and temperatures drop. The forest takes on a more sombre colour and on a still winter day the forest almost seems asleep. You may walk on forest ridges at times like these when the only noise will be the sound of your own feet and even this will be muffled by beds of moss. In the gullies, streams filled by the winter rain tumble between mossed boulders and archways of fern.

Kamahi Blossoms — *Weinmannia racemosa*
Kamahi is one of the most common forest trees. It occurs on North, South and Stewart Island, in montane forests from the Waikato south. In some areas it becomes the dominant tree thereby creating podocarp-kamahi communities and in places like Stewart Island and Mount Egmont replaces mountain beech as the sub-alpine forest species. In sheltered valleys it may be 21-27m tall but in sub-alpine situations the canopy is considerably lower and wind shorn. Kamahi belongs to a genus of about 100 species confined to the Southern Hemisphere. New Zealand has two species of Weinmannia: *kamahi and tawhero.*

Tawari Flowers — *Ixerba brexioides*
The Maoris called the flowers whakou and strung them into necklaces and garlands. This is appropriate for it is a beautiful tree and flowers during two of the nicest months of the year — November/ December. Tawari is a bush or canopy tree 6-16m tall growing in the montane forest of North Auckland and south to Rotorua and Lake Waikaremoana.

Mingimingi —*Cyathodes fasciculata*
All but two of the eight New Zealand species of Cyathodes *are endemic. Worldwide, the genus contains some 175 species spread throughout Australia, Tasmania, Polynesia, New Guinea, Malaya and New Zealand. Mingimingi is a shrub up to 5m tall with small flowers which are viewed properly only through a hand lens. It is found on the Three Kings Islands and the North and South Islands, in coastal to lower montane scrub and light forest from near North Cape to mid-Canterbury.*

Clematis — *Clematis paniculata*
The New Zealand clematis flowers are white, green or yellow, whereas the clematis flowers of other countries include brightly coloured species. Clematis paniculata is a liane common in lowland and lower montane forests in North, South and Stewart Islands. There are some 250 clematis species mainly from temperate regions.

Lichens

Lichens are invariably the first plants to colonise exposed rock surfaces but in the forest they have many other places to grow. Lichens are made up of fungal and algal partners living together and creating a wide variety of forms.

They have no seeds, grow very slowly, (about 1mm per year), can exist only on a fixed surface and reproduce vegetatively. The hyphae of a developing fungus spore captures a few cells of either the green or the blue-green algae. In some way this stimulates growth and the lichen begins to develop. The algal partner may be one of over 30 species which live free in nature, while the fungal partner is never free living. The alga, unlike its fungal partner, must have sunlight for photosynthesis and requires sufficient organic food not only for itself but for the fungus as well. Most of the mineral requirements are supplied by rain. While the alga is little changed by its association, it can only reproduce by cell division. Unlike many plants in the forest lichens are less sensitive to changes of temperature and humidity and can thus withstand long droughts.

Lichen — Baemyces fungoides

This scientific name means little fungus although the plant is actually a lichen and the little growths shown here arise from the fungal partner. The lichen occurs in Australia, Tasmania and America as well as in New Zealand. It is commonly found on open clay banks where there is plenty of light but seldom direct sun. This photograph was taken in early April.

Tunnelweb Spider — *Porrhothele antipodiana*

Related to the trapdoor spiders and the tunnelweb spider of Australia, this species is not dangerous to humans. The up and down movement of its fangs is confined to this group of spiders but is inadequate protection against the shiny black wasp — Priocnemis (Trichocurgus) monarchus, which hunts and kills it. They are found in podocarp forests under stones, in rotten logs and hollow trees; where they construct a bulky silken tunnel or tube which is 2.5cms diameter and up to 25cms long. The tunnel entrance opens on to a silken web which no doubt acts as a signalling device on the approach of insects. Once caught, an insect, usually a beetle, is dragged back into the tunnel and eaten, the remains being neatly sealed off with silk at the tunnel end. The two-three hundred eggs laid by the female are loosely wrapped in a sac and hatch early/ mid summer. The young stay with the female for some time before leaving and probably take two to three years to reach maturity.

Ground Orchid — *Thelymitra longifolia*
Although probably the most common of the twelve New Zealand species of Thelymitra *it is often hard to find a flower fully open. The flower photographed was the only one among hundreds in this locality caught open after three seasons of sporadic searching. It occurs among rocks, on banks and open ground from montane to sub-alpine situations throughout North, South, Stewart and Chatham Islands. It is also found in Australia, Tasmania and New Caledonia.*

66

Virgin Podocarp-Hardwood Forest

*This photograph shows a part of the few remaining hectares of virgin podocarp-hardwood forest. There are no mammals of any description here and it is a unique opportunity to compare the present day forests with the forests which once clothed much of our country. The first feature striking a visitor is the deep bed of humus on the floor and the heavy growths of moss and lichen. They act as a large sponge, helping forest plants to withstand drought and preventing excessive rain run off. The second feature is that plant species which have been largely eaten out of neighbouring forests by browsing animals grow here in abundance. They include three species of astelia, mountain five finger, mistletoe and the larger-leafed coprosmas. Unlike the neighbouring forests the unpalatable species do not dominate and the undergrowth is not full of hookgrass —*Unicinia sp., *and the prostrate tree fern —* Dicksonia lanata.

Rewarewa (Honeysuckle) — *Knightia excelsa*

Rewarewa is one of New Zealand's two members of the protea family which worldwide contains some 50 genera and over 950 species. Most occur in South Africa and Australia. Rewarewa is regarded as one of the ancient elements of New Zealand's flora. It occurs commonly throughout the North and South Islands and as far south as Marlborough Sounds in lowland and lower montane areas. The tall tree which grows quickly, attracts nectar feeders such as bellbirds which help to cross-pollinate the flowers.

Hinau Flowers —*Elaeocarpus dentatus*
As a canopy tree it grows to 15m with a trunk up to 1m in diameter, but on forest margins and in land reverting to forest, it flowers while a much smaller tree. It is distributed from sea level to 600m throughout North and South Islands. In pre-European times the Maori used the fruit to make a type of bread and extracted from the bark the ingredients for tattooing pigments.

Orchid — *Dendrobium cunninghamii*
The largest arboreal orchid in the forest clings to the bigger forest trees by roots specially adapted to absorb moisture from the atmosphere. The flowers, which are dependant on insects for pollination, are often difficult to see because the plants are perched so high. The minute seeds are dispersed by wind. Dendrobium cunninghamii *belongs to a genus of nearly 1,000 species distributed throughout* India, Ceylon, Southern China, Japan, southward through Malaya, Pacific and Australia. This species is endemic and grows on well-lit tree trunks and branches in the North, South and Stewart Islands.

68

Northern Rata Blossoms — *Metrosideros robusta*

The minute wind blown seeds lodge in the boughs of large trees. It is some years before this epiphyte's aerial roots reach ground level and penetrate. Eventually, the roots grow to a massive size, encircling and killing the trunk of the host tree and in time they create a trunk of their own sometimes 2m in diameter and up to 30m high. It grows on coastal and lower montane areas in the North Island and the top end of the South Island.

Rata Tree

North Island Kiwi — *Apteryx australis mantelli*
This kiwi lives only in the North Island. Kiwis are nocturnal forest dwellers, well known for their long bills with which they obtain worms and other food in soft ground. When feeding they plunge their bills into the ground, sometimes up to their full lengths. They have poor eyesight but have developed tactile bristles around the mouth, which combined with the sensitive bill, help the birds to move around the forest. This bird, being hand held, was photographed in daylight and fell asleep in the keeper's hands. They are seldom seen in the wild although reasonably common in some areas.

Tararua — South Ohau
Damp and protected valley floors like this one abound in the Tararua Range.

Kiwis, cuckoos and kakas

As the forest cover retreated, the number of birds diminished. Contrasting with the migratory cuckoos are the flightless kiwis with wings reduced to small useless appendages completely hidden from view. All five kiwi species, unique to New Zealand, are nocturnal and remarkable for the fact that they are the only birds with nostrils in the end of their bills. They are also renowned for the huge size of the egg, compared with the size of the bird itself. The kaka, a large forest parrot, is also confined to New Zealand. It is a strong flyer and although not as abundant as formerly, can still be found in places like the Kaimanawa and Tararua ranges. Its diet of fruits, including matai, miro, tawa, kauri and kahikatea berries, must have aided the dispersal of podocarp forest in the past. Smaller parakeets, kakariki, are possibly a little more plentiful but even so their chattering is not heard as much as formerly.

The tui, the most notable songbird in the forest, aids pollination as it draws nectar from flowers, some of which seem to be adapted for pollination by birds; consider the irregularly shaped flowers of kowhai, flax, and puriri. An interesting feature of the tui is the collection of hairs on the tip of its tongue. This small brush helps in the collection of nectar.

The saddleback, stitchbird and native thrush have disappeared from the mainland completely. The kokako, falcon and weka are vastly reduced in numbers. The laughing owl and native quail are extinct. In spite of this decline we can still enjoy the songs of the bellbird, greywarbler and tui, or the sighs and chatter of smaller birds like wrens, riflemen and fantails. Only two kinds of birds have increased in numbers in the last century. The silvereye, self-introduced from Australia, has the Maori name of Tauhou — stranger. The blackbird was introduced in the early colonial days and is the only introduced species to adapt thoroughly to dense forest.

It is the lack of birdlife, the absence of mammals and the stature of the forest which on a still day creates the cathedral-like peace. There is a total lack of animal warmth so evident in forests or jungles elsewhere. The number of species has declined since the European arrived but what effect this will have on the future ecology is uncertain.

Kiekie — *Freycinetia banksii*
Kiekie is New Zealand's member of the pandanus or screw pine family that is normally associated with the tropics. It is a climbing shrub frequently ascending tall trees by large brittle roots. On the ground it can form tangled masses and fill small gullies so that they are almost impossible to penetrate. The leaves which are 45-90cms long have a sharp serrated edge which has earned it the name cutty grass in some areas. The sexes are found on different shrubs. Flowers are found about September/October and the fruits ripen in May. The plant grows on both main islands down to latitude 42° in the east and to Fiordland in the west. It grows most luxuriantly in the northern areas. See also page 43.

Moth — *Asthena subpurpureata*
Delicate and nocturnal, this little moth is found in the same localities as a similar species, Asthena pulcharia. The other species is a pale blue-green colour rather than grey-brown but otherwise they look alike.

Land Snails — *Paraphanta traversi*
New Zealand supports more than 370 different species of land snails most of which are between 1-15mm long. Two large genera have unfortunately been reduced by wild pigs since their introduction. The large species are very localised in some cases. It is thought that their global dispersal probably occurred in Cretaceous times. The group Paraphanta is one of a primitive southern carnivorous family ranging from South Africa to Melanesia including 42 species and subspecies.

Primitive frogs and vegetable caterpillars

Many of the plants and animals which are unique to New Zealand are also rare, small or nocturnal so that many people are unaware they exist. The native frogs are a good example.

They are of a very primitive type and in the main confined to small local areas on a few mountain ranges and islands. They do not live in water but are kept sufficiently damp by rain, dew and mists which often shroud the hills. These nocturnal animals lay eggs in clusters under rotting logs or loose stones and the tadpoles develop into frogs while still contained in a gelatinous capsule. When the tiny tail-wagging froglets emerge they have bypassed the free-swimming tadpole stage. It is however the skeletal structure which makes them unique among the world's amphibia.

In the podocarp-hardwood forest flanking the lower slopes and foothills of Mount Egmont the so-called vegetable caterpillar is found. When taken from the ground the caterpillar is a solid wooden corpse with a shoot up to 15cm long protruding from its head. This is what has happened. The caterpillar, while alive, eats the microscopic spores of a fungus — *Cordyceps robertsii*. The growth of the fungus fills the whole caterpillar from which it draws its nourishment. Thus while retaining the shape of a caterpillar it is gradually converted into a hard object. When this is complete a shoot develops behind the head bearing spores that are shed to set the process in motion again.

Many moths but few butterflies

It is estimated that New Zealand supports some 10,000 insect species but there are no native honey bees. Before the introduction of the European wasp, flies were much more numerous. There are few butterflies but hundreds of moths. One is tempted to find some connection between these factors and the general insignificance of many native flowers. Brightly coloured or highly scented flowers evolved to attract either insects or birds to aid pollination. Since nearly all the moths are nocturnal, colours, showiness and size may be less important. This is speculation and it remains for researchers to find a true answer.

The relationships between plants and insects and between different insects continues to be probed and undoubtedly many fascinating discoveries are still to be made. While photographing some of

72

Mixed Podocarp-Beech Forest, Tararua Ranges

The Tararua Ranges contain many types of plant community. In this picture one can see mixed podocarp-beech forest in the foreground, dense stands of beech on the ridges and alpine grasslands on the rugged tops.

Squeaking Longhorn Beetle —
Hexatricha pulverulenta
This attractive beetle is common in some areas during September. The larvae which grow in the bark of a wide variety of dead trees are parasitised by an ichneumon wasp.

New Zealand Pigeon *Hemiphaga novaeseelandiae novaeseelandiae*
Pigeons are common forest birds which play a major role in distributing the seeds of forest trees. While it eats the leaves of many forest plants it also eats berries including fuchsia, puriri, wineberry, tawa, podocarps, matai, supplejack, nikau, and karaka. The birds are easily approached but when disturbed fly off noisily. They are strong flyers, covering large distances sometimes at a great height.

Weka *—Gallirallus australis*
The weka, one of New Zealand's flightless birds with only rudimentary wings, was formerly widespread. All 4 sub-species declined in numbers dramatically after European arrival and although the cause is not known for certain is thought to have been disease. They live in dry scrub country and on the edge of forests, can run very fast and will swim without hesitation. They are omnivorous. They also mate for life.

Cicadae — *Amphipsalta*
With a wing span of 7cm this is the largest cicada in New Zealand. The loud chirping song heard on hot summer days is made only by the male and in some seasons the noise can be deafening. They are harmless to humans but cause damage to some plants. The female lays eggs on twigs forming a herring-bone pattern with her ovipositor as she does so. On hatching the minute cicada nymphs fall and burrow into the ground where they feed on the juice from plant roots. The length of time they spend in the ground is not known but it is at least three years. A North American species spends seventeen years in the soil before emerging as an adult.

At least twenty one species, all of which are endemic are found in New Zealand and in each species the males use a different song to attract their mates. Special sound producing structures occur under the abdomen and are particularly noticeable in the male. The song is also aided by the rattling of the rigid wing membranes. The Maoris ate the developing nymphs and liked the insects because they heralded spring.

Weta — *Hemideina thoracica*
This wingless member of the grasshopper family is one of our best known insects. It emerges at night and makes a scraping sound familiar to most people. There are many different weta species throughout the New Zealand region, some of the offshore island varieties measuring up to 25cm long. The males, as they grow, develop much larger heads and bigger mandibles, while the females can be easily distinguished by the long ovipositor. They feed mostly on rotting vegetable matter and contrary to common belief do not possess a sting. A nip from a fully grown male can however be a little painful and break the skin. When provoked they bring their hind legs over their body as in this photograph, drawing them suddenly downwards and backwards. This movement produces a rasping noise. The large species are clumsy and retiring insects which seldom jump, while the small species can jump long distances.

Forest Gecko —*Hoplodactylus granulatus*
This gecko can be found in both podocarp and beech forests as well as scrublands. They are distributed throughout the North, South and Stewart Islands where they live in the treetops and feed on insects. The forest gecko is quite common although often difficult to detect because of its camouflage markings and ability to change its colour through a range of shades. The inside of the mouth is bright orange. When fully grown they measure up to 20cms long. In warm weather they sun themselves. It is thought that like all New Zealand lizards, they were much more plentiful before the introduction of rats.*

77

Lowland forest

In areas of podocarp-hardwood forests where there is moist fertile soil tree ferns flourish. In this locality, Urewera National Park, beech trees mingle with the podocarps and many plants familiar to both beech and podocarp-hardwood forests are present. The area is sheltered from strong winds but receives frequent rains.

Rata Vine — *Metrosideros fulgens*
This rata vine occurs on Three Kings Island and in the coastal and local areas of the North and South Islands. It is often confused with the northern rata (Metrosideros robusta) which strangles its support. This rata by comparison is a liane up to 10m or so long with the main stem approximately 10cms in diameter. In the past, the inner bark was used to heal the sores and stop bleeding or sometimes boiled with the bark of the kauri and rimu to make a lotion for the sore backs of horses.

Stick insects —*Acanthoxyla sp.*
All the New Zealand species of this harmless vegetarian are wingless. Some have smooth bodies, others especially the larger species have spines. They feed during both day and night on tender shoots and leaves where their shape camouflages them against the attack of predatory birds. Lost limbs are easily regenerated although the new ones do not usually grow to their original length. Many species have both males and females, but some consist only of females, whose eggs develop by parthenogenesis into more females. With bisexual species, both sexes can develop from fertilised eggs.

Daybreak in the Southern Tararua Ranges

Dracophyllum latifolium
This tree grows up to 7m tall and is confined to the North Island between latitudes 35 to 39 degrees. An odd-shaped tree, refer the two photographs shown, it has long but thin branches bearing leaf tufts at the end which lend a strange character to the forest. The Maori name is Nei Nei.

Collospermum microspermum
Usually an epiphyte but occasionally growing on the ground, this plant is found only in the North Island. The other endemic species, Collospermum hastatum has a wider distribution. Only four species are known, the other two occurring in Samoa and Fiji.

81

Tawa — *Beilschmiedia tawa*
*Tawa belongs to the laurel family
comprising about 1,000 species mostly of
tropical origin. Cinnamon, camphor and
clove nutmegs are all obtained from
members of this family. Within the family
there are about 40 species of the genus
Beilschmiedia. Again, they are mainly
tropical although the two New Zealand
species, tawa and taraire are endemic.
Tawa is a forest tree 30m tall and with a
trunk 1m diameter, often forming the bulk
of the forest in a tawa-podocarp
community. It grows from sea level up to
800m. Large trees may be up to 400 years
old although 200-300 years seems to be
more common. (A. E. Beveridge)
Depending on age, the degree of exposure
and growing space, the shape of trunks
and crowns can vary greatly.*

the smallest flowers I have seen minute insects emerge. The tree putaputaweta is remarkable in its powers of regeneration. The larvae of the large ghost moth riddle the trunks with holes while a different insect attacks the smaller twigs creating woody bulges. In spite of these attacks the plant thrives. It is not unusual for the empty tunnel to be occupied by a weta, hence the plant's name.

Types of podocarp-hardwood forest

Depending on where the forest is located, one or other of the large tree species dominates. Hence we have podocarp-hardwood forests with different characteristics. The most dramatically dominant tree in the north is the kauri. These massive trees rise unbranched from the floor to a height of up to 50 m, dwarfing all other plants in the community. It is thrilling to walk amongst these giants and sobering to realise that much of the Auckland peninsula was once clothed with kauri forest. The wasteful milling of the kauri forest in the 19th century has ceased. Usually in close association grows the taraire, so that if the kauri is absent owing to fire or felling, taraire becomes the dominant tree.

In other areas, tawa *Beilschmiedia tawa* dominates, so the name tawa forest is used. Where rimu is present in quantity the forest takes its name but it is usual to find other podocarps present as well. Similarly, totara forest contains other podocarps but generally occupies dryer

ground. In this case either totara *Podocarpus totara,* or Hall's totara — *Podocarpus hallii,* is present. It is unusual to find concentrations of matai so the term matai forest is unlikely to be appropriate.

Kamahi forests, characterised by the large amount of kamahi, cover wide areas. As it is frost-tolerant the forest grows on Mount Egmont to an altitude where it assumes the form of sub-alpine forest and appears as far south as Stewart Island in similar conditions. If you follow the Mount Egmont road to the Stratford Mountain house you can visit the "Goblin Forests" — gnarled kamahi trees draped with beards of moss and crusts of lichen. Kamahi is probably the most common large tree in the country and in lowland regions reaches a canopy height far greater than in colder situations.

Rata forest contains many specimens of either the northern or southern ratas which have thrust their irregular shapes above the canopy. Dead ratas often stand for many years supporting large growths of epiphytes.

The final forest type warranting mention is the kahitatea or semi-swamp community. As the name indicates, the ground is too wet for many forest plants. Kahikatea is often the sole tree but, depending on the amount of water, other plants may be present. What the podocarp-hardwood forest lacks in brilliance it compensates for in subtlety. Where colour is lacking, patterns substitute.

Toe toe — *Cortaderia fulvida*

There are four species of toe toe in New Zealand, all four growing in the North Island but only two being found in the South Island. They are the largest endemic grasses but should not be confused with the widely cultivated pampas grass of Argentine. The toe toe flower stalks and plumes are neither as long nor as erect as the pampas.

Kauri Forests

The largest remaining area of kauri forest is Waipoua State Forest. Only 2632 hectares, this forest contains both mature kauri and stands of kauri rickers or seedling trees. The southern limit known as the 'kauri line' runs from Tauranga past Matamata, Te Aroha, Huntly and out through the Kawhia Harbour. North of this line there were once 1.6 million hectares of kauri forests. It is by far our biggest tree, the massive trunks normally being 3 metres diameter but reaching 7 metres and growing 30 metres high. Occasionally specimens tower 50 metres above the forest floor. Kauri forests tend to be dryer than normal podocarp-hardwood forests, and although many podocarps and associated plants grow in the same community it is the sheer bulk of the kauri which dominates. The untapering trunks may rise branchless to a height of 18-21 metres; the massive branches often support large epiphyte growths. Mounds up to 4-5 metres high form at the base of the large trees as a result of bark shed over several hundred years. The trees are thought to grow for over 1,000 years maybe 1,500. Kauri is cone bearing and belongs to the family Araucariaceae which includes the monkey puzzles. The genus of about 15 species occurs also in the Philippines, Polynesia and Australia.

Nikau Palms — *Rhopalostylis sapida*
*New Zealand is the southernmost outpost
for the palm family of over 4,000 species
and supports only one species. It grows in
the Kermadec, Raoul and Sunday Islands
reaching down to Banks Peninsula on the
east and Greymouth on the west. For some
reason the southern nikaus tend to be
taller than northern specimens reaching
26m in the south and about 15m in the
north. The southern plants are also
hardier although plants are more common
in the northern regions where they lend the
forest a tropical appearance. Regeneration
is profuse under the cover of other trees
but does not occur in the open.*

Totara Flats
*The grassed area of Totara Flats in the
Tararua Ranges provides relief from the
surrounding forest. Alpine scrub and long
growing beech trees frame the foreground
while the podocarp forest and species are
confined in the main to the valleys. On the
flats themselves are the remains of large
totaras which were killed by natural
causes long ago.*

Rain in the hills
*A consistent supply of rain throughout the
year is vital for the survival of our
podocarp-hardwood forests. Rainfall
varies considerably from area to area
however because of changing topography.
The forests have ways of retaining water,
including spongy moss, the humidity
beneath the canopy, and roots in the soil
but cannot withstand long drought. In the
summer of 1974/75 trees began to die in
some areas. Dense rain forest occurs
mostly where moisture laden winds off the
sea strike mountain ranges. On average
there are only small differences in
rainfall between seasons.*

sub-antarctic forests

Parakeets chatter in the crowns overhead. One nips off a leaf and watches it spiral to the floor; another strips twigs off a small branch. They chatter softly as if constantly checking on each other. It is mid-morning and they have eaten well. Close by a flock of tiny riflemen run up and down the beech trunks in search of insects making barely audible sighs as they move between the forest giants. Over on the ridge a flock of bush canaries noisily hunts calling continuously as they search the upper canopy for food. They are scared for a moment by a pigeon which lands heavily amongst them but return to feeding almost as quickly as they left. Sharing her time between the floor and the upper canopy a fantail chases air-borne insects dancing in the air as she follows a moth's irregular flight. With tail fanned she perches in time to see a robin lunge at an intruding robin from the neighbouring territory and drive it back over an invisible boundary. It is winter, the forest is damp and the beech leaves have lost the flush of spring green. A light breeze ruffles his feathers as he sits hunched in the limb of a silver beech. The falcon is satisfied for now, having eaten a pigeon which he struck out of an old beech several metres away. Then he rolls noiselessly off his perch and with quick flaps of his wings rises above the canopy uttering a repetitive scream which causes nearby birds to hesitate. But he circles the forest ignoring the flock of parakeets which has launched for the other side of the valley. Back on the forest floor a robin scratches among the leaves for insects, confident that there are no predators to disturb his peace.

Tararuas —Waiohine Gorge
Beech forest merging with podocarp forest occurs in many North Island localities. The gullies and valleys are heavily mossed, crisscrossed with fallen trees, and tangled with lianes, while the ridges are fairly open. The area in the photograph has never been milled. The Waiohine river in the distance, like many mountain rivers can rise very quickly after heavy rain, but falls equally quickly when the rain ceases.

Beech forest interior

This photograph is an attempt to show the original condition of beech forest undergrowth which in pre-European New Zealand was not at all easy to penetrate. Browsing animals have greatly thinned out the understory, trampled the floor and selectively eliminated the palatable plants. In recent years photographs showing park-like beech groves with little except beech leaves covering the floor have been published. While these situations are very attractive they should not be confused with the appearance of virgin forest. It is true however, that some virgin forests supported more undergrowth than others depending on rainfall and soil type. The plants growing in the understory usually include the springy coprosmas, bushlawyers and ferns, but there are generally fewer species. Compare this photograph with the undergrowth in a podocarp forest to see the difference.

Beech forest is quite different in appearance and atmosphere from the "jungle" of heavy podocarp-hardwood forests. Whereas the podocarp-hardwood forests usually occupy good quality soils, beech forests can tolerate poorer soils and much drier sites. Temperature change does not seem to be important. There is no beech on Mount Egmont or Stewart Island and only isolated patches north of Auckland. Scattered beech trees occur widely in the North Island although heavy concentrations are found in Fiordland, West Coast, Northwest Nelson, and the ranges of the lower North Island. Areas of almost pure beech forest include Fiordland/West Coast, North/West of the South Island and the Rangitaua forest where many of the accompanying photographs were taken. Many forested areas today could be described as podocarp-hardwood beech forest because they contain a mixture of species. Owing to this range of intermediate forest some with more podocarp species and others with more beech and associated species, this section illustrates some of the purer beech forests in order to demonstrate the greatest contrast.

Like all forests, they have shrunk since man arrived. Beech forest formerly grew on some areas of the Canterbury Plains, but repeated burning by early Maoris combined with a climatic change have caused tussocks to dominate. Because it grows on poorer soils and in harsher sites beech forests has suffered less than podocarp-hardwood forests from the axe and fire of European man. In fact over two-thirds of our remaining native forests contain beech trees or are dominated by one or other of the beech species. The purest natural forests in New Zealand are probably dry mountain beech forests of inland Canterbury where few other species grow.

Only seldom are all beech species found together in one place, a notable exception being Western and Central Nelson. The number of species in the undergrowth increases with rainfall and the appearance of beech forest is greatly influenced by altitude. In lowland regions the canopy is 30-37m high but at the other extreme on poor sites near the bush line beech can be reduced to a stunted shrub 1.5m tall. Obviously the plants and animals living in either situation have very different conditions to deal with.

92

(a)

(b)

(c)

Beech species

Hard beech   — Nothofagus truncata (a)
Black beech   — Nothofagus solandri (b)
Red beech   — Nothofagus fusca (c)
Silver beech — Nothofagus menziesii (d)

There are four main species of beech as illustrated. A fifth, mountain beech, used to be treated as a separate species but it is now simply regarded as a variety of black beech by most authorities. The leaves and bark of all the beech trees vary enough to make identification easy, if it weren't for the fact that all except the silver beech hybridise in the wild.

The shapes of beech trees vary enormously depending on altitude, the exposure to wind and whether they are growing singly or in a forest. The forest trees have taller trunks and the branches are concentrated in the crown while a beech tree growing in the open develops a more conical shape with large branches closer to ground level. It has been suggested that the changes in leaf size reflect a progression from moist to dry conditions but the distribution of the species does not bear this out. There are some twenty species of beech found in New Guinea, New Caledonia, Australia, temperate South America and New Zealand where all four species are endemic. Beeches are evergreen but nutrient deficiencies cause leaf colour changes some of which have been photographed. The tiny flowers are wind pollinated.

93

Green Gecko — *Naultinus elegans*
Measuring only 20cm long when fully grown this gecko had a special meaning to the old time Maori. The mouth is bright blue inside and the species has a remarkably loud "bark" as a means of defence. It was the bark which concerned the Maori who believed if he heard the bark of a kakariki, a relative would soon die. This gecko is found only in the North Island throughout scrublands and forests. As far as we know it feeds on insects. During winter months, due to the cold, it is inactive only becoming active again when the warmer weather returns. Small red mites which suck the lizard's blood are often found around the eyes of geckos as well as on wetas and some moths. This species uses its prehensile tail as a fifth leg when climbing the forest canopy.

Tararua Ranges — *Marchant ridge*
Silver beech Nothofagus menziesii, *dominate many high ridges in the Tararua ranges. Because of high wind, they do not grow as tall as they would in sheltered gullies or valleys. Moisture laden clouds and frequent rain enable heavy growths of moss and lichen to cover the trunks and branches. The growths do not harm the beech trees. After a spell without rain these mossy growths become dry and brittle but act like a sponge at the first rain shower. Being on high ridges they get rain even when the lower ones don't. In winter, water can be squeezed out of the moss with ease.*

South Island Robin —*Petroica australis australis*
Although unrelated to European robins the three New Zealand species are equally inquisitive and have strong territorial instincts. This South Island species is found on some Cook Strait Islands and in Marlborough, Westland, Western Otago and Southland.

All of the robins are insectivorous and hop around the forest floor turning over leaves and flitting after moths or winged insects. They are plentiful in some areas particularly where stoats and weasels are trapped. There are signs that the North and South Island species are invading second growth scrub and exotic forests.

Astelia solandri
Of the twenty five odd species of Astelia most of which are found around the Pacific, thirteen are confined to New Zealand. Astelia solandri grows as a tufted epiphyte on trees but also on the ground in the wetter lowland forests of North and South Islands. On large trees such as the northern rata it grows into heavy masses and like many epiphytes stores water in the thick curved bases of its leaves.

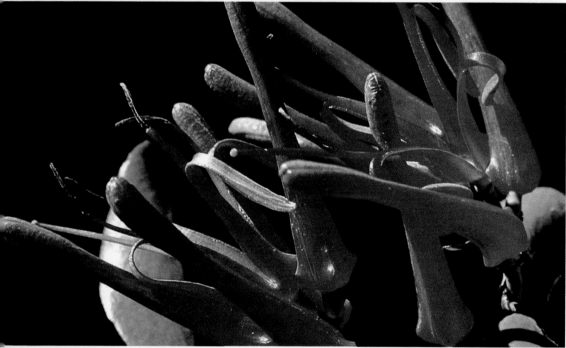

Crimson Mistletoe —*Peraxilla colensoi*
This beautiful parasite, one of two endemic species, grows on silver beech and occasionally on species of rata or pittosporum. Once widespread and well-known to the Maoris and European pioneers, it has been so reduced that many present day New Zealanders do not know that it exists. At the turn of the century people in beech forest areas collected it at Christmas time for decoration. In one such area I talked to older people who remembered mistletoe but yet took one week to locate flowering specimens. The plant now grows on introduced species such as Pyrus, Robinia and Rosa. It is found in the North and South Islands. The flowers vary in colour to some extent.

Lawyer — *Rubus cissoides*
This lawyer, one of the five endemic species, belongs to a cosmopolitan genus of about 1,000 species. This is the same genus as the blackberry and raspberry and the similarity of the berries shows this. The berries have a pleasant taste and were preserved by early European settlers, while a sweet juice which dropped freely from cut stems was drunk by bushmen. Inpenetrable masses of this liane grow over trees and shrubs climbing by means of the prickles to a height of about 15m. Depending on locality there is tremendous variation in the shape of the leaves. It occurs on Three Kings, North, South and Stewart Islands where it is common in lowland and montane forests.

Ichneumon Wasp — *Netelia producta*
Although featured under "Beech Forests" where this specimen was found it no doubt occurs on podocarp-hardwood forest as well. The little red wasps which do not have a sting harmful to human beings are common during summer months, and are attracted to electric lights during hours of darkness.

Millipedes
Contrary to common belief millipedes do not have 1,000 legs. They have two pairs of legs for each body segment while their close relatives, the centipedes, have only one pair. Millipedes are herbivorous feeding mostly on rotting logs and living roots, while centipedes are carnivorous. They are common throughout forests, most of the species being less than 5 cm long.

Cave Weta — *Gymnoplectron longipes*
Cave wetas are most active on moonless nights when they emerge from their dark and humid caves, or crevasses, onto surrounding foliage for 2-3 hours. They have no wings, small jaws, eyes and bodies, but long hind legs and antennae. It is the sensitive antennae and mouth parts which enable them to move swiftly in the dark. Despite their appearance they are not aggresive although they are subject to cannibalism during mating or just after moulting before the exoskeleton has had time to harden. Cave wetas are well represented in New Zealand with fiftyone known species. There are more to be described; a large number of these are endemic. They are considered to be members of an ancient group of insects with fossils dating back 190 million years.

Fiordland National Park
The beech forests of Fiordland National Park contain red, silver and mountain beech. Red beech is confined to the valleys while the other two species grow in a wide variety of places. Fiordland is one of the world's largest national parks covering 1,223,890 hectares, some of which are still virtually unexplored. Much of the forest clings to the steep rock faces only by a shallow layer of peat and humus which in a dryer climate would not provide adequate rooting space.

Ruapehu water fall
Water falls are common on the western flanks of Mount Ruapehu. There are many small plants which seem to concentrate close to the water courses, growing in seepages, within the spray of waterfalls and on stream banks. It has been suggested that the water, originating in the snow and ice, absorbs minerals on its way down the mountain and it is these dissolved minerals the plants seek. Ourisias, sphagnum moss, ranunculas, various orchids, parahebes, and epilobium are among the smaller plants found in these situations.

Green Clematis — *Clematis foetida*
This plant climbs by means of tendrils to a height of about 6m and flowers in October. It grows in lowland forests in both the North and South Islands, especially on the forest edge.

Natural hybrids

For a long time beech identification appeared complicated and it was only within the last 50 years that botanists discovered that all the species except silver beech cross naturally in the wild to create numerous intermediate forms. The most common crosses are between black beech and hard beech, and red beech and mountain beech. The foliage and bark of the hybrids indicate the parent species.

Within the beech forest

Compared with the podocarp-hardwood forest true beech forest contains few tall trees other than the beech. The canopy, from above, is much more uniform and without the emergent podocarps and ratas so characteristic of other forest types. Within the shelter of the canopy there are big differences too. There are fewer tree ferns, and virtually no lianes or shrubby epiphytes. As less light penetrates the canopy, the undergrowth is not as dense and has fewer species; mostly regenerating beech seedlings. The forest floor is usually more even with fewer filmy ferns and mosses, although there is often a thick moss carpet of *Dicranoloma* species. In Fiordland, with high rainfall, the trees are festooned with mosses and lichens while dry beech forests are far less luxuriant. With little over half as many plant species as lowland podocarp-hardwood forests, this forest assumes a cleaner, more restrained beauty.

Morchella Sp.

It is best to treat all fungi as poisonous unless you have an expert knowledge of them. This specimen was photographed in the Rangitaua forest in October when the ground was damp and mature beech trees sheltered the forest floor from direct sunlight.

Spider webs

Spider webs found throughout all forests are constructed mainly after dark although the spiders will begin during daylight hours if the day is dull or overcast. Not all of the threads laid by the spiders are sticky; some are positioned purely to reinforce the web. Towards the end of constructing a web the spider lays an even coating of a sticky substance on the silk. This sticky coating gathers like a string of tiny beads as the silk stretches. The web's centre. where the spider usually sits, is free of the substance, although the spiders don't become tangled in their own webs because of their protective coating of oil which they constantly renew. Naturally as insects are caught the webs become damaged. Some spiders may use the web for several days but others tear down the damaged threads and rebuild every night. Not all the species of spiders in New Zealand construct webs like this.

Moth — *Azelina gallaria*
This moth is one of many cryptically coloured and shaped, making them difficult to see unless they fly. I have watched one dislodged from a tree in daylight simulate a falling leaf and spiral to within a few metres of the forest floor before flying to shelter of nearby bark. This action to avoid predators, would not occur in darkness.

Lake Rotoroa — Nelson Lakes National Park

Separated from Lake Rotoiti by the 2,000m high Travers range, the two lakes were originally formed by glaciers and are more than 76m deep. Today they act as the twin sources of the Buller river. Beech forest is found throughout the 57,136 hectares of the park and fringe the lakes to the water's edge. The photograph shows the Sabine river flowing into the lake.

Forest Lichen — *Beard "Moss"*

Old Man's Beard is one of the 40-50 species growing in New Zealand belonging to the genus Usnea. *Identification of species in this large genus is often difficult because so many similar forms exist. Most species, including the one photographed, live on trees and shrubs. They are found at the forest edge exposed to full sunlight and do not grow in the forest interior. Colours range from grey green to deep yellow.*

Fiordland Mist

Cloud and mist add significantly to the amount of water which is available to plants in forests. This is particularly important to epiphytes especially the mosses and lichens which are so common in Fiordland. It is estimated that some parts of this forest receive over 700cm of rain each year. During winter months of course some of this falls as snow. We have therefore two factors, cold and abundant water which determine what plants and therefore what animals can live here.

Although rainfall in most mountain areas is inadequately measured because of the difficulties encountered in steep remote country, it is known that only small differences in rainfall occur with seasons and that the highest rainfall occurs where winds flow directly from the ocean into the mountains. In pre-European New Zealand the ground cover was untrampled by browsing animals and it is certain that a thicker floor covering held a greater supply of moisture for forest plants.

Blechnum penna-marina
*There are about fifteen New Zealand
species in this genus of some 200 species
which are distributed mainly throughout
the Southern Hemisphere. Very common in
the beech forests of the volcanic plateau, it
is found in the North, South, Stewart and
Chatham Islands as well as in South
America and some sub-antarctic islands.
It grows from sea level to sub-alpine
conditions.*

104

Umbrella Fern — *Gleichenia cunninghamii*
The umbrella fern is common on the edge of beech forest, on stream banks and in clearings where it sometimes covers several square metres.

The umbrella fern family of 130 southern and tropical species is divided into six genera, three of which are represented in New Zealand. They frequent the drier places such as savannahs and moors of tropical and sub-tropical countries. The Maoris called this fern Tapu-wae-kotuku (the footprint of the white heron). It is found only in New Zealand but occurs abundantly from North Cape to Cook Strait as well as a few local places in the South Island. The other member of the family illustrated in this book is Gleichenia circinata found in sub-alpine regions.

Crown Ferns — *Blechnum discolor*
These ferns can measure as much as 1.5m across and are often raised on a short trunk. They are abundant in open forests from sea level to 900m where they can cover large areas of floor to the exclusion of similar sized plants. Found on all main islands, they also grow in the Auckland and Campbell Islands as well as Tasmania and Australia.

Kaka, kakapo, kakariki

The forest is home to many birds although sadly, some beautiful and interesting species are now either reduced in numbers or very rare. At the top of such a list comes the large nocturnal ground parrot, the kakapo, which is struggling to exist in remote parts of Fiordland. Here in the steep-sided glacial valleys it has survived while in other areas where it was once common it has vanished. In the beech forests as well as in the podocarp-hardwood forests, the strong flying parrots, kaka, and kakariki also survive, but although they are managing better than the kakapo, are few in numbers.

Within the forest shelter robins, pied tits, fantails, riflemen, grey warblers, tuis, bellbirds and the bush canary live. Two birds, the yellow headed bush canary and the closely related brown creeper, are found only in the South Island beech forests or along its margins. During spring both long-tailed and shining cuckoos invade the forests, hawks and falcons hunt over the canopy while kiwis and moreporks feed at night.

Most of the small birds feed on insects and crustaceans which they catch on the wing or under leaves on the forest floor. The nectar-seeking birds such as the tui and bellbird can be heard squabbling in thickets of tree fuchsia or in summer amongst the beautiful mistletoe flowers. In winter when flowers are absent honeydew which grows on the small beech twigs becomes an important food.

One bird famous for the fact that the male and female have different shaped bills occurred in ranges where beech was common. It is the extinct huia which when observed in the days of early European colonization shared the chores of food collecting. The male with his stout powerful bill broke open rotting logs while the female with her long and curved bill probed for insect larvae out of reach to the male.

Starred Gecko — *Heteropholis stellatus Confined to the beech forests of the northern South Island, this lizard is very similar to the green gecko* — Naultinus elegans, *although when mature measures only 15cms long. Like all New Zealand geckos it gives birth to young, whilst all other members of this worldwide family lay eggs. This species like all of our geckos invariably gives birth to 2 offspring.*

106

Red Crowned Parakeet — *Cyanoramphus novaezelandiae novaezelandiae*
Now very rare on the mainland this pretty parakeet is confined to large areas of forests in both main islands. Although seldom seen, they are often heard chattering in tree tops or flying swiftly over the forest canopy. The rapid chattering call Ki,Ki-Ki-Ki-Ki-Ki-Ki is made only when flying and is replaced by a more relaxed conversational chattering when the parakeet is perched. They feed on a wide variety of fruits, seeds, leaves and buds. There are several closely related sub-species on small offshore islands.

Virgin beech — Fiordland
Overall the forest exists today as it did hundreds of years ago. There has been no milling in the area and the undergrowth is mainly beech seedlings. Waterfalls cascade off the very steep mountains in all directions, especially during wet weather.

Dart Valley

The glacier formed Dart Valley still has a glacier at its head which feeds the Dart river. The mountains on both sides of the valley are capped with permanent snow and clothed in the lower reaches and almost vertical sides with beech forest. In the foreground a spaniard grows in the sub-alpine tussock, while in the distance a waterfall tumbles out of Lake Unknown which fills a high cirque between Mounts Nox and Chaos. The waterfall disappears in winter when the lake is frozen.

The flowering and fall

As with all evergreen forests the seasons are far less marked than in deciduous forests. In winter the canopy is a uniform dark green breaking into a brighter green with new spring growth. Only mature beech trees flower, between the months of September and November, producing small reddish flowers which are wind pollinated and in good years produce clouds of pollen. The male and female flowers while separate are found together on the same twig.

Seeding follows flowering with the seedfall reaching its peak in March and April when much of it is eaten by birds. The trees do not flower every year and the frequency varies between species, good years being most frequent in silver beech and least frequent in mountain beech. In a good year however, mountain beech may produce up to 49 million seeds per hectare (Source J. Wardle).

Leaf fall, not associated with autumn, occurs in hard beech towards the end of August when dark green leaves turn yellow green. Many leaves turn yellow before the spring leaf fall and the appearance of flowers. By October when most of the leaves have fallen the ground under hard beech is littered with yellow leaves. As the seasons move into winter the forest returns to its more sombre tones.

Seedling thickets

Beech seeds which fall to the floor usually wait until the following spring to germinate. The resulting seedlings need overhead light but a little shade in order to grow. Seedlings can survive for many years making little headway until a gap appears in the canopy. Some seedlings, it is estimated, have grown only 152mm high in 20 years because they lacked sufficient light. Once a mature tree dies or falls to the forest floor seedling growth accelerates to as much as 91cm a year and in a relatively short time a dense thicket of seedling beech has formed preventing further seedlings from becoming established. It will be 80-120 years before the fallen tree is replaced with another mature one. The maximum ages of beech trees varies between species being about 600 years for silver beech, 550 years for red beech, 500 years for hard beech, 400 years for black beech, and 350 years for mountain beech (Source of material: J. Wardle).

Eglinton Valley

The oldest rocks of the valley were originally sandstones and limestones laid down on the sea floor between 300-400 million years ago. The sediments which were very thick, became hardened with pressure and folded by forces in the crust. This caused the rocks to recrystalise resulting in the schists and gniesses of Fiordland today. The folding took place about 200 million years ago accompanied by intrusions of melted igneous rocks such as granite.

At a much more recent time the valley was scoured by a glacier which left the three glacial lakes of Gunn, Fergus and Lockie as the ice retreated. Today the Eglinton river flows for 40km on the broad valley floor. The Earl Mountains on the west and the Livingston mountains to the east are composed of volcanic rocks and hard granites. Now beech forests clothe much of the floor and the valley sides.

Hollyford Valley — Fiordland National Park

The uniform nature of mature beech forest is well illustrated here. In a similar area of podocarp forest more species would comprise the canopy through which mature podocarps would emerge. Here in the Hollyford Valley, Fiordland heavy growth of moss and lichen clothe the beech trees.

Koromiko — *Hebe stricta*
The greatest number of Hebes species is found in New Zealand where all but two of the many species are endemic. There are seventy nine named hebes, many varieties, a great deal of hybridization and more still to be described. This makes identification difficult. There are four varieties of Hebe *stricta the most common of the koromikos. It is a common plant of up to 4m high growing on lowland and lower montane areas in scrubland, open places and forest margins in the North Island. It is represented in the South Island by a similar plant.*

Astelia nervosa
Rare north of Auckland, Astelia nervosa *forms considerable colonies in some mountain and sub-alpine forests. It is also found on tussock grasslands although it adopts a smaller habit there. The berries can be seen from December to at least March when this photo was taken. It occurs in the North, South and Stewart Islands.*

wetlands and water communities

The sun is high. Insects hum and tuis swing drunkenly on the flax heads as they draw nectar from the blossoms. Silvereyes dart between stalks while a fantail returns with a crop full of insects to her young. She lands in a manuka bush near the edge of the swamp and fills the gaping mouths inside the neat conical nest. In the swamp amongst the raupo a tall bittern stalks for food; insects, water snails, small birds and nestlings if he can find them. He is startled. His sharp heron-like beak points upwards as he adopts a camouflage posture. He is almost impossible to see as his plumage matches the colour of the dead raupo blades and his markings obscure his outline. A water hen or pukeko has landed close by to begin foraging. She walks stealthily catching insects and eating the soft shoots of the water plants which she holds up to her bright red bill with her foot. The whole atmosphere is relaxed, humid and sweetly scented. Even the harrier hawk now at the end of the swamp, circles effortlessly.

The wetlands and water communities include streams, lakes, swamps, bogs, damp courses and bog forest. In pre-European times they were much more extensive than they are today although they were never as dominant as the forest. They occur at all altitudes, those of the coastal and sub-alpine regions being referred to elsewhere. The more acid wetlands carry Manuka or *Dacrydium* scrub. Sphagnum bogs are found mainly in the south where alpine bogs and tarns are common. Swamps however, are confined to the lowlands.

Life in New Zealand water communities is more restricted than in other countries. There are no native water frogs. Of the 28 main groups of insects, 10 have aquatic representatives although all of these except the water beetles/bugs live above water as adults and only spend their young stages in the water. The plants are neither showy nor exist in great variety. As so many plants and animals cannot tolerate excess moisture, the constant presence of water creates new communities.

Lowland swamps

Swamp vegetation consists mostly of tall and medium-sized grasses and rush-like plants. There are several types of swamp which, like all communities, constantly change. One is the raupo swamp which occupies soils of many types but which needs a very wet floor. Often there is little else growing in the centre of the swamp although flaxes, toetoe and manuka will invariably grow on the margins. As the swamp ages, humus from the raupo blades builds up and the swamp becomes dryer. Another main swamp type is the flax or *Phormium* swamp which as the name indicates, contains a lot of flax. This is nearly always the large flax-*Phormiun tenax*, which grows very tall. In spring the distinctive flower stalks attract nectar seeking birds in large numbers. Amongst the flaxes and grass live the swamp hen — pukeko, bittern and small rails, although the latter two are seldom seen as they are well camouflaged and not very common anyhow. The dryest swamp is the shrub or manuka swamp where, as the name indicates, shrubby plants have

Flooded forest

When water is dammed and the forest becomes flooded, the trees die quickly. In this situation beech trees suffer. Ducks, kingfishers, shags and the occasional heron now inhabit the shallow lake which in its sheltered water supports mats of the floating red fern-Azolla rubra. Native water vegetation is neither as showy nor as plentiful as in other countries.

Grey Ducks — *Anas superciliosa superciliosa*
The Grey Duck is one of the more common native ducks occuring throughout New Zealand although like all the inland water birds, its numbers have decreased as swamps and waterways have been modified. It feeds on plant and animal matter by upending or dabbling in shallow water. Nests are generally constructed away from water frequently in a tree fork or hollow tree. Eggs are laid between September and December and incubated by the female. In recent times the Grey Duck has hybridised naturally with the introduced Mallard Duck, the Grey drake more readily mating with the Mallard duck than the Mallard drake with the female Grey. As a result there are few pure Grey Ducks or Mallard Ducks left.

Scented Sundew — *Drosera binata*
The sundews are mostly bog plants, many of them occurring throughout Australasia. This species which grows in boggy ground in the North, South, Stewart and Chatham Islands has scented flowers which bloom from November to February. Some plants living in bogs often find it difficult to get the nutrients necessary for growth and to overcome this have evolved means of catching and digesting insects. The sundew leaves are covered with clubbed, glandular hairs, each one bearing a drop of sticky fluid at its end.

As an insect touches the hair, it becomes glued and other hairs bend towards it to secure it further. This triggers off a further secretion, which has a function similar to human gastric juice. In a few days all but the insect's exoskeleton has been digested.

Sphagnum Moss
The four New Zealand sphagnum mosses form a distinctive moss group although even experts have difficulty distinguishing between varieties, forms and species. Sphagnum grows, usually in extensive bogs from 1900m to lower altitudes, in areas where there is a degree of acidity. The plants grow closely together forming soft hillocks and cushions of spongy moss and rely on rain water to keep the plants moist. As the upper parts of the plant grow the lower part dies but, owing to the lack of oxygen, does not decay. In a very dry summer a sphagnum bog may become dry enough to catch fire. The bogs which occur widely often support other plants but the species present vary tremendously with locality.

established. In any one swamp all three types of plant can occur depending on the nature of the land and the depth of water. Of all types, the raupo swamp can be the most difficult to explore because the intruder is often supported on a floating and submerged mat of vegetation through which he can break at any time.

If the swamp dries sufficiently the forest trees invade but if the soil is acid bog plants become established instead. Where there are open areas of still water the small floating fern, *Azolla rubra,* forms red mats. The growth can be so continuous that at a quick glance it could be confused with a neatly kept lawn.

Bog vegetation

Areas with high rainfall, frequent cloudy skies and comparatively low summer temperatures favour bog development and for this reason they are most common in the west and south of the South Island and Stewart Island. Sphagnum moss is a constant feature of bogs although the associated plants vary according to altitude, location and surrounding vegetation. Bogs only occur where soil is saturated all year round; sphagnum occupying the wettest places and scrub the driest. Scrub-bog like scrub-swamp contains manuka with small plants growing in their shelter. A sphagnum-fern bog has fern and sedges forming an upper layer while low-growing species like lycopodium grow in the sphagnum mat.

Semi-swamp forest

By far the most dramatic wetland community because of the very tall trees and buttressed roots is the kahikatea forest which occurs in the lowland belt throughout the country although absent from North Otago and Stewart Island. It is a distinctive community which reaches its greatest development near rivers which overflow their banks. Unfortunately nearly all the northern kahikatea forest has been destroyed, the largest remaining areas now being in South Westland. As one moves from North to South the plants which make up the forest alter. Because the floor is too wet for any normal forest plants they must perch on fallen trunks. The epiphytes of course are unaffected as they are well above water level.

The appearance of kahikatea forest is different from anything else in New Zealand. There are many kahikatea reaching up 30m and very occasionally 60m. They grow close together with large buttressed roots frequently standing in pools of water. The crowns have scant foliage and in the North Island clumps of *Astelia solandri* grow in the forks. Many shrubs grow in the understory and there are often large tangles of kiekie. Normal forest birds and insects can live in these forests although mosquitoes tend to be more numerous because of surface water.

Bog forest

Much less dramatic and generally confined to small areas, bog forest is dominated by one or other of the podocarps like silver pine-*Dacrydium colensoi* or yellow pine-*Dacrydium intermedium.* These bogs are usually located in montane regions and have a dense undergrowth of astelias, phyllocladus and coprosmas. The trees are seldom more than 12m high.

Swamp — Urewera

There is probably no other type of vegetation which has been so modified as the swamps. In many areas they are drained or filled in. This swamp in the Urewera National Park is surrounded by virgin forest and has only a few square metres of open water. The rest of the area supports large growths of sphagnum, plenty of stunted manuka and many sundew plants. At the swamp margin on more stable ground grows New Zealand flax, cabbage trees and toetoe. Only plants adapted to very wet condition can tolerate excess water. Aeration is often poor in waterlogged places and plants have modified their structure to ensure that the oxygen requirements of their roots are satisfied.

Manuka/tea tree — *Leptospermum scoparium*
Manuka is a very common widely distributed and highly adaptable plant. When it grows in exposed windy positions, it assumes the form of a prostrate plant only a few cms high. In sheltered places, it grows into a tree up to 7m in height. It is usually associated with change, colonising river flats, landslide debris and volcanic ash and also in such divers situations as swamps, coastal dunes and mountains.

There are some 35 species in the genus most of which are Australian but three of which are endemic to New Zealand. It was called tea tree by European settlers because bushmen literally made a bitter tea from its leaves. There are number of garden varieties with beautiful coloured flowers. The white blossoms of this species occur in December and January.

Raupo — *Typha orientalis*
Raupo swamps usually contain water too deep for many plants. They occur in marshy places throughout the Kermadec, North and South Islands supporting fewer species in the southern areas.

silence and solid water

The forest is quiet and even though the day is calm a cool breeze draughts the forest which bears a simplicity and crispness never matched by lowland vegetation. The canopy presses close and as the leaves of nearly all the trees and shrubs are small, less light reaches the mossed floor. There is little birdlife. A grey warbler trills somewhere in the canopy and a bellbird silently slips through the twisted branches. Spider webs which span the spaces between many plants glisten in the shafts of sun which penetrate the understory. Blowflies swarm over a dead bird. A kea calls loudly its cry echoing in the rock couloirs above the forest. Winter has yet to come and by then the smaller birds will have retreated to the lower altitudes.

An archipelago of alpine islands stretches from East Cape southwards to Fiordland isolated from each other by an ocean of warmer lowlands. Here sandwiched between the level of perpetual snow and the upper limits of the forest lies one of the richest alpine floras in the world. In the seemingly inhospitable climate of the alpine and sub-alpine zones over 900 different plants live in a surprising abundance and diversity. The beauty of the lowlands and the drowsiness of the warmer coasts is replaced with a grandeur and vigour which sets the region completely apart.

Many plants and animals cannot survive the transition to alpine life and so we are faced with a change of species so startling that nearly all that we have discovered in the lowlands must be forgotten and new conditions understood. During the ice ages alpine vegetation covered many low-lying areas but as the ice retreated and the forests reclaimed the land, the alpine environments become isolated at higher altitudes. This provided opportunities for separate plant development and so we have closely related, yet quite distinct species growing on small mountain areas and confined in some cases like Mount Egmont to a single mountain. This separate plant development has enriched the flora and resulted for instance in many species of mountain daisy and buttercup.

An alpine influence must have been working in New Zealand for a very long time because whole genera are confined to New Zealand. Very few large animals make a permanent home here as the breeding season is shortened by the early arrival of winter and summer activity is reduced to a few months. Even so, some are specially adapted and, like the grasshoppers, are found nowhere else. Almost half of the native plants in New Zealand occur in the alpine zone where the greatest variety is found in the South Island. About 71% of all the alpine plants are confined to the greater mountain area of the South Island while the North Island has only a few species not found elsewhere. Overall there are hundreds of species which never descend to the warmer lands, about 100 which occur at lower altitudes only under special conditions and many species common to both zones. Of the purely alpine plants about 93% are found nowhere else.

(Source: A. F. Mark and Nancy M. Adams, New Zealand Alpine Plants).

The chief factor limiting plant growth seems to be the average amount of time that snow lies on the ground. Snow which falls at any time can flatten vegetation and high winds which buffet the foliage, illustrate the new set of conditions to which the plants have been adapted. Frosts occur at all seasons of the year. The soil is often very cold reducing the flow of water to the leaves. At other times the soil is warmer than the surrounding air, the intensity of sunlight increases with altitude and dry-moist periods can follow each other quickly. Additionally avalanches are not uncommon so these alpine plants have to withstand violent wind, drought, temperature change and the flattening impact of snow and ice.

It is hardly surprising that the plants are low growing and are modified to withstand conditions which lowland plants never experience. Out of 500 high mountain species 138 are between 15cm to 31cm high: 199 are less than 15cm high and 92 are less than 5cm high.

(Source: L. Cockayne, NZ Plants and Their Story, 4th Edition).

Every region, in fact every mountain, forms an environment peculiar to itself because of the nature of the rock, the slope, and the amount of rain. On any one mountain there are different sites on which plants can live; some situations fed by rain or snow melt favour plants needing moisture, while well drained scree slopes favour other species. The tolerances accepted by alpine plants are often very narrow so that species moved from one location to another will no longer flourish and may die altogether. Just as the plants in the forests alter as one moves either south or north so do the plants in the alpine zone.

Erratic weather

Overall the alpine flora acts as a huge sponge protecting the lowlands from the excessive run-off. As any mountain climber knows, the erratic weather on mountains can virtually bring all seasons into conflict in a single day. There are few consecutive frost-free days per year. Temperature data published on the Old Man range in Central Otago for instance shows less than 75 frost-free days per year, over

100 days when ice remains solid and the balance of year best described as freeze-thaw days. As for rain and snow, the amount and the duration vary considerably over short distances. Even so we know that most moisture precipitates on the western slopes and that fog which often surrounds high peaks adds humidity and moisture to the soil. The alpine area above the bushline on the Tararua range receives over 500cm of rain per year, Mount Egmont 731cm per year, and Arthurs Pass township about 396cm per year. (Source: A. F. Mark and Nancy M. Adams, NZ Alpine Plants).

The puzzle of alpine flowers

Many plants such as the anisotome, pimelia, astelias and spaniards are unisexual and need to cross pollinate, while others such as *Cyathodes, gaultheria* and *gentians* have bisexual and female plants thus encouraging cross-pollination yet enabling all plants to produce seed. (Source: A. F. Mark and Nancy M. Adams, NZ Alpine Plants). The buds of most alpine plants develop in Autumn and lie dormant through the winter

Kea — *Nestor notabilis*
Although most often seen about the mountain beech bushline keas are essentially forest birds. As they are more easily seen above the bush line, the impression that they live there persists. While it is the only alpine parrot in the world, it shelters in the forest during heavy frosts and snow fall often feeding on the forest floor in winter. They spend a lot of time in the treetops but nest on the ground under boulders, in crevices, hollow logs and among tree roots. The nest is usually near the forest edge but seldom in cold places such as near a stream or in a narrow gorge. Keas eat insect larvae, roots, flowers, berries, whole plants like anisotome and help by spreading the seeds of many alpine plants. They have also learned to treat carrion as food and are widely believed to have become a predator within the last 100 years. While some keas do kill sheep it is estimated that they attack only one out of 20,000 sheep in the high country.

Sub-alpine forest

As the altitude of beech forests increases the number of plant species decreases and there is a gradual merging of montane and mountain beech. Here the canopy is low with few emergent trees and rounded by fierce winds.

months. When spring arrives the flowers bloom within a few weeks and can therefore take advantage of the short growing season in the warmer months.

Nearly all discussions on the New Zealand alpine region refer to the lack of colourful flowers. It seems that owing to the lack of long tongued bees and butterflies, pollination is carried out by moths which are nocturnal plus flies and beetles which are numerous in the short alpine summer. There is no lack of scent and as the plants appear well adapted to the pollination by these insects coloured flowers offer little advantage.

The sub-alpine forests

The high mountain forests occupy much the same area today as they did in pre-European times. They have suffered less than the lowland forests mainly as they were more difficult to reach and because they often occupy high rainfall areas which were less attractive to European settlers clearing the bush for pasture.

As illustrated in the photographs of the beech forest interior shown, the trees are low and twisted with gnarled growth. The mature beeches are clothed with moss and lichens, lianes are few, tree ferns are absent, shrubby epiphytes are rare and the undergrowth of twiggy shrubs like coprosmas fairly light. The upper limits of sub-alpine forests vary greatly with latitude, the bush line being roughly 1450m in the Kaweka ranges, 1200m in the Tararua ranges and 900m in Fiordland. This illustrates that the further south we travel, the lower the bushline descends. Also the distance from the ocean affects the temperature and therefore the altitude of the bushline.

The types of trees creating sub-alpine forest vary with locality, being kamahi on Mount Egmont, silver beech in the Tararua ranges and mountain beech in most other ranges.

Sub-alpine forest occurs from East Cape southwards often separated from the tussock grass by a band of scrub. The sub-alpine beech forests can be either wet or dry communities, fewer associated species of course growing in the drier forests. On the floor grow hook grasses-*uncinia sp*, lycopodium and cushions of moss which may completely

Mountain Beech — *Nothofagus solandri var. cliffortioides*
This is now regarded as a variety of the black beech, N.solandri, *The leaves are more pointed and the trees, because they grow at high altitudes, have a much lower stature. Mountain beech forms the dominant tree up to the bush line in most sub-alpine forests, the Tararua range where silver beech replaces it, being one of the exceptions. The mountain beech bark is smoother and the wood paler than black beech.*

Kaikawaka — *Libocedrus bidwillii*
The high montane and sub-alpine forests of some areas contain mountain cedar. Its pyramidal crown and yellow-green foliage contrast with the rather sombre green and rounded canopy of the mountain beech. The stringy bark has few lichen growths which by comparison can completely smother the beech trunks. The dead cedar in this photograph illustrates its shape.

Milford cirque

Carved by glaciers, thousands of years ago the characteristic u-shaped valleys are now lined with vegetation. On the upper edges alpine plants thrive. There is an abundant supply of water during the warmer months because not only does the mountain supply constant streams of snow melt but the high Fiordland rainfall ensures 625cm a year. After a heavy rain the steep valley sides are transformed into thousands of waterfalls. The alpine plants growing in the Fiordland cirques include senecios, mountain daisies and buttercups. The alpine scrub species include coprosmas, hebes and olearias.

bury the larger tree roots. The under-scrub consists of sapling beech trees, coprosmas, fivefingers and mountain toatoa. In wet forests, the undergrowth is denser and contains more species including the umbrella fern, mountain cedar, broadleaf and snow totara.

The sub-alpine kamahi forests contain no beech although there are other trees such as mountain cedar and mountain toatoa. In some areas the cedar and mountain totara dominate a community while in the south, southern rata communities become a feature. Montane and sub-alpine bog forests can occur in any of these situations and are formed where the ground is wet through poor drainage.

Sub-alpine scrub

Merging with the stunted forest and the open grasslands, sub-alpine scrub marks the beginning of the true alpine zone. Trees no longer grow tall at this altitude and the sub-alpine scrub is sometimes little more than stunted beech or kamahi about 1m high. Well developed scrub comprises hebes, coprosmas, cassinias,

senecios, dracophyllum, and gaultherias.

Most people think of scrub as a regenerating nuisance of hard-to-penetrate manuka covering land which could be better used. The alpine scrub however, is a garden carefully created by nature and fulfilling an important protective role. The scrub flowers, for the most part white, are generally small, but the variety of leaves, shades of green and shape of the plants more than compensate.

Here even more than in the forests, the plants are exposed to strong winds and heavy snow falls. There is also frequent rain during all seasons which leads to a soil rich in peat and humus. The scrub which is entirely absent on some mountains forms a wide band, on others gradually decreasing in height as altitude increases until it finally gives way to plants, better able to withstand the conditions. There are various types of scrub community, any one of the following plants tending to dominate in a single locality; mountain toatoa, dracophyllum, manuka, beech, cassinia, and olearia or bogpine.

Leatherwood — *Olearia colensoi*
*Well known to trampers in the Tararua
and Ruahine Ranges, leatherwood grows
as a wide band of sub-alpine scrub. It is
springy, hard to penetrate and the leaves
have a rough toothed edge. It is found in
the North, South, Solander and Stewart
Islands. Towards the southernmost part of
its range it grows almost to sea level.
There are 32 New Zealand* Olearia *species
and a number of varieties listed in the
New Zealand Flora. The genus contains
about 130 species distributed mainly in
Australia and New Zealand with a few on
Lord Howe Island and New Guinea.*

Alpine Toatoa – *Phyllocladus alpinus*
*Alpine toatoa occurs in sub-alpine forest
and scrub on both main islands as well as
the lowland forest of Westland. It is a very
common constituent of scrub merging with
sub-alpine forest on the one hand and
tussock on the other. It grows to a tree or
shrub up to 9m tall which has a habit of
layering as the lower branches curve
downwards. What appear to be the leaves
are actually flattened branchlets which
serve the same purpose as leaves and
which are thick and fleshy. The whole
plant is very aromatic even the dried
leaves having a strong scent. The true
leaves are minute and rudimentary. Cones
appear from October-January depending
on altitude and locality. The two other
species, in the genus, tanekaha and toatoa
are lowland trees.*

North Island Mountain Senecio —
Senecio bidwillii
All but one of the 40 New Zealand Senecio
*species are endemic. They belong to a
cosmopolitan genus of over 1500 species.
This species,* Senecio bidwillii, *has two
varieties one of which is confined to the
South Island. It occurs in montane and
sub-alpine scrub where the thick leathery
leaves are well able to stand inundation by
snow and strong sun in summer.*

Mountain Pinatoro — *Pimelia prostrata,
var. erecta*
*The world-wide Daphne family of about
500 species has 15 representatives
endemic to New Zealand. This mountain
form is one of the 80 species in the genus
Pimelia which occur in Australia and New
Zealand. The species has great variety of
forms some of which are true breeding,
others which are merely habitat
modifications.*

Tongariro
*A most inhospitable place, yet alpine
plants are colonising lava flows less than
twenty years old. Because the area drains
quickly in dry weather, most of the plants
are adapted to withstand periods of
drought. Within the confines of this
photograph there are several different sites
in which plants grow. In the background
are loose scree slopes inhabited only by
plants with special ability to withstand
moving stones. A mineral spring marks the
beginning of Mangatepopo stream which
has cushions of sphagnum moss in places
along its banks. There are soggy areas
filled with bog plants and yet only several
paces away are plants growing in well
drained soil or volcanic debris which often
need to survive drought conditions during
the summer months.*

Nurseryweb Spider — *Dolomedes minor*
*Photographed on sub-alpine scrub which
in winter months can be snow covered this
species is found over large areas of New
Zealand in scrub and long grass although
never in a deep forest. The spider is
nocturnal and very sensitive to vibrations.
When hunting the adult actually pounces
on an insect which is crushed into a small
moist ball and turned over and over.
Digestive juices are secreted and the fluid
contents of the insect sucked by the spider
for a period of 10 minutes after which the
indigestable remains are discarded. In late
spring and early summer the females can
be seen carrying egg sacs about while
hunting. Just before the baby spiders are
due to hatch the female fixes the sac to a
shrub or tussock and spins a nursery web
around it. She stays with the web for about
seven days while the young hatch within
the protection of the web. Here they
remain for about one week after which
they escape through small tears which
have developed in the nursery walls.*

127

Alpine scrub
The scrub may consist of leatherwood, dracophyllum, mountain toa toa, stunted mountain beech, hebes, gaultherias, coprosmas and pimelias depending on the location and the mountain range. Many of the scrub plants also grow within the sub-alpine forest and mix freely with tussock. On some mountains such as the northern Tararuas, wide bands of leatherwood make progress slow and uncomfortable. I have been in scrub so thick that I walked in the crowns rather than through it and then only with some difficulty. Altitude and high winds make it impossible for trees to survive.

Sprawling Coprosma — *Coprosma cheesemanii*
As with all coprosmas the fruits are more attractive than the flowers. Coprosma cheesemanii is a sprawling shrub which grows in permanently damp, often peaty sites in tussock grassland or herbfield and in open sub alpine scrub from Mount Hikurangi southwards to Stewart Island.

128

Tall grasses and pigmy pines

The sub-alpine scrub usually merges its upper limits with alpine grasslands as the tussock communities are by far the largest in the mountains. There can be either tussock or mat grasslands but either type needs more fertile soil than fellfield, which we will explore soon, and grows best on clay where it builds up humus. The higher the rainfall, the greater the number of species which invade the tussock.

Fully developed tussock, usually snow grass or red tussock, is very dense, making it difficult for other plants such as herbs to enter. Mixing with tall tussock in some places where the ground is damp or even boggy is one of the world's smallest conifers, the pigmy pine — *Dacrydium laxifolium*. It seldom grows more than 25cm high, but has sprawling branches up to 1m long.

Celmisia gracilenta

This genus of alpine daisies is centered in New Zealand where 58 endemic species occur. They are among the most common and easily seen flowers in the alpine region. While flowers are very similar between species the leaves display marked differences. Natural hybridisation occurs between species. This graceful little daisy grows in both the North and South Islands on lowland and lower montane grassland as well as herbfield and bog.

Greenhood Orchid — *Pterostylis australis*

Cross pollination in this genus is enforced by a plant mechanism which traps an insect once it is inside the flower, making it crawl over the stigma and out over the pollenia to gain its freedom. The genus of some 60 species occurs mainly in Australasia with a few representatives in New Caledonia and New Guinea. Several of the 19 New Zealand species are common to Australia. Pterostylis australis occurs only in the North, South and Stewart Islands and probably on all of the wetter mountain ranges.

129

Tussock — *Chionochloa*

The snow tussocks of the Australasian genus, Chionochloa, *contain some 20 species and are concentrated in New Zealand. Several of the 14 alpine tussocks are local but others are very widespread. It is impossible to imagine the lower alpine regions without them because they are the dominant plants over wide areas. In the area on Mount Ruapehu where this silhouette was photographed, tussock merges with mountain beech, mountain toatoa, snow totara, gaultheria, lycopodium, senecios, and hosts of other plants. Tussocks provide shelter within which more delicate alpine plants like the harebell-* Wahlenbergia albomarginata, *can grow. The tussocks themselves are very hardy although they can be quickly damaged by browsing animals. Many insects, particularly grasshoppers and butterflies are conspicuous in the summer months.*

130

Alpine Gentian — *Gentiana patula*
Most of the 24 New Zealand species are mountain plants although one grows in the coastal rocks of Foveaux Strait and another on the Chatham Islands. Closely related forms occur also in Tasmania. The genus is widespread but typically alpine. Many of the overseas species are richly coloured while the New Zealand species are mainly white. *Gentiana patula* grows in the North and South Islands in sub-alpine grasslands from the Tararua Ranges southwards although it is rare west of the main divide near Nelson. It is among the last alpine flowers to bloom, flowering between January-April.

Red Tussock — *Chionochloa rubra*
As the common name indicates this tussock has a distinctly reddish tinge not emphasised in this photograph because of the back lighting. It grows on both main islands as well as Stewart Island in lowland and low alpine regions up to 1,500m. Red tussock is common on the volcanic mountains of the North Island and on the mineral belt of Nelson-Marlborough and Otago.

Tussock lands

In all alpine areas of New Zealand there is a marked contrast between the upper limits of the forest and the alpine zones. In the space of a few yards the forest gives way to tussock or alpine scrub. On some mountains the band of alpine scrub is wide while on others it barely exists and the transition to tussock is abrupt. In the Tararua ranges there are large areas above the bushline clothed in tussock. During the winter tussock lands are often buried under snow.

Celmisia hieracifolia
This celmisia with leathery leaves grows in the North and South Islands on a wide range of situations including sub-alpine, grasslands, herbfield, and even the margins of fellfield or debris slopes.

Mount Aspiring National Park
The slopes of Mount Earnslaw on the right, with permanent snow and the peaks of the Barrier Range in the distance are now part of the Mount Aspiring National Park. The foreground tussock is above the bushline which in this area occurs at roughly 1,200 metres. There is virtually no scrub here as the mountain beech forest opens directly on to tussock resulting in a parklike setting absent from many mountains. In the shelter of the tall tussock grow many mountains herbs. During some winters the entire area down to the valley floor is covered in snow with deep drifts persisting in the tussock long after it has melted at lower altitudes.

Grasshoppers — *Sigaus piliferus*
This grasshopper photographed on Mount Ruapehu has a wide variety of colour forms from green, yellow and dark brown through to a deep red. It occurs widely in sub-alpine scrub, herbfield, tussock and on the stony fellfield. In all of these habitats it is difficult to see unless disturbed as its colouring so perfectly matches its surroundings.

All of the New Zealand grasshoppers, with one exception, have abbreviated wings and do not fly; they range in length from less than 2cm to nearly 5cm. Most of the species are alpine or sub-alpine and only one species is found in the North Island. Very little is known about the life cycle although one species is said to reach maturity in two years.

It is thought that the ancestors of New Zealand alpine grasshoppers have been adapted to cold climates for a very long time, maybe 100 million years. Their nearest relatives are restricted to cool environments in Tasmania and Chile. All except one of the 15 New Zealand species so far described cannot descend to the lowlands and are in effect confined to their alpine islands. Grasshoppers are usually more diversified and abundant in warmer climates.

Desert Road
The eastern side of Mount Ruapehu, called the Rangipo Desert, and shown at left below, contrasts dramatically with the western side which is heavily forested. Here constant winds dry the soil and have removed much top soil. Tussock can be seen growing on pedestals of earth indicating that surrounding soil has been stripped away. Also on this side of the mountain is a sulphurous river, the Whangaehu, which spills from the crater lake and scours the soft volcanic earth. In spite of this there are clumps of tussock, hebe, gaultheria, and Dracophyllum *as well as smaller alpine plants such as gentians which survive.*

Dracophyllum recurvum
This small dracophyllum is important and widespread in the central volcanic region. It is confined to the central and eastern mountains from sub-alpine to high alpine situations in the North Island where depending on the degree of exposure it forms a low growing mat or a semi-erect shrub. While all of the New Zealand species are endemic not all occur in the alpine zone, some growing in montane forest. Dracophyllum recurvum *hybridises naturally with* Dracophyllum filifolium *and* Dracophyllum longifolium.

Tangle Fern — *Gleichenia circinata*
Unlike many ferns in the umbrella fern family it is abundant in swampy places up to about 1300m. It occurs in both New Zealand and Tasmania where it forms carpets covering hectares of damp sub-alpine land bordered by tussock and sub-alpine scrub.

Snow covered Celmisias
Alpine plants must be able to withstand violent changes. Frosts occur at all seasons, winter snows lasting many days can bury plants in several metres of snow, violent winds are common, rain and mist are frequent, the soil is often extremely cold and yet on still sunny days there is intense heat due to clear skies and altitudes. As a result the growing and flowering season is short and many alpine plants have thick leaves or special structures to help them withstand these conditions. So well have they adapted in fact, that they cannot tolerate richer soils and milder climate of lower altitudes as many would be gardeners have discovered. The greatest favour you can do an alpine plant is leave it alone.

136

Mountain Gardens

Beautiful alpine gardens occurred on all of New Zealand's mountains prior to the introduction of browsing animals. In spring and summer depending on locality the low growing alpine vegetation will be flowering. Many alpine plants are confined to relatively small areas on some mountains. In the bottom photograph Dracophyllum recurvum *and* Gaultheria colensoi *are seen growing out of a mat of moss. The white moss is* Rhacomitrium lanuginosum.

Common Spaniard — *Aciphylla squarrosa*

The seedling leaves of the spaniard are quite soft and grasslike while the adult leaves, up to 1m long are stiff and have sharp tips. The flower stalk, shown close up here, is 60cm-2m tall and the flowers faintly scented. Aciphylla is one of the most distinctive and important alpine genera with 40 species, all except one of which is confined to New Zealand. Although some species have a restricted distribution the species shown here occurs from Mount Hikurangi southwards to central Canterbury.

In the alpine zone it grows alongside streams and on wet or shady banks or depressions in mixed tussock and snow tussock grassland. The spines have not developed as a protection against browsing animals which were absent from early New Zealand, but are a modification to help the plant to withstand drought. The plant yields a semi-transparent gum which gave the Maoris one of their most prized scents.

North Island Edelweiss — *Leucogenes leontopodium*

The edelweiss is so common in such places as the Tararua ranges that they grow like daisies on a lawn. The two endemic New Zealand species are similar in appearance to the Swiss Edelweiss-Leontopodium alpinum. The North Island species grows on sub-alpine and alpine sites on rocky ground and rock crevices from Mount Hikurangi southwards, although the South Island species does not occur north of Cook Strait. There is some evidence of natural hybridism between edelweiss and Raoulia species.

Dracophyllum pubescens
A prostrate shrub, it is confined to the South Island mountains of Western Nelson, North Westland and the main divide southwards.

Herbfield — Buttercups and daisies

Herbfield occurs in the high mountains where there is frequent rain and the surface allows the accumulation of humus and peat. The best herbfield is found on the mountain passes of the Southern Alps and the floors of glacial cirques. There are several types of herbfield, one mixing with tussock and another with sub-alpine scrub. In a fully developed herbfield the plants grow close together. Within a small area during spring and summer occur buttercups-*Ranunculus*, hare bells-*Wahlenbergia*, native foxgloves-*Ourisia*, eyebrights-*Euphrasia*, Maori onion-*Bulbinella*, spaniard-*Aciphylla* and gentians. In damp places the alpine cushion-*Phyllachne colensoi* and the alpine fern-*Gleichnia circinata*, cover the ground. Both the buttercups, which were described by early botanists as "the finest in the world" and the daisies, *Celmisias*, are seen in all herbfields. The plants growing together on a herbfield vary between dry and wet mountains and between the North and South Islands.

The flat topped mountains of South Otago and Stewart Island are ideal for herbmoor and alpine bog which grows there over large areas. The herbmoor is covered with matlike growths of phyllachne, raoulia and *Dracophyllum muscoides* among which are dotted celmisias, senecios, buttercups and low growing hebe. Snow often persists here well into summer and the water which drains slowly in the peaty soil is always cold.

The alpine bogs nearly always contain Sphagnum moss, sedges, rushes and the alpine fern-*Gleichnia circinata*. On the bog surface, among other plants, grow the pigmy pine, sundews, cyathodes and bladderwort. While neither herb moor nor bogs are as common or cover the areas which the herbfield and tussock cover, small areas can be found on many mountains.

White mountain Daisy — *Celmisia incana*
Growing singly or in large mats, the white leaved mountain daisy is found in montane and sub-alpine grasslands, herbfield, and rocky places in both North and South Islands. It is conspicuous because of its regular silvery-white foliage which clothes many well drained sites. The leaves of many celmisias have an aromatic fragrance.

Nelson Lakes National Park — Hopeless Creek catchment

In winter the whole area is buried in snow and the tarn which supports no obvious water life is frozen. While some of the surrounding slopes are stable, others are continually moving. On a quiet day in summer, visitors to the area can frequently hear rocks ricochetting down steep gullies and crashing on to the rock and shingle fans. Many alpine plants including vegetable sheep, gaultherias, tussocks, spaniards and ranunculus grow on the stable slopes.

Only lichen lives on the exposed rocks below a small hanging glacier. The air is clean and a light breeze strokes the mountain. Apart from the stream which trickles from the glacier face there is no sound. Nothing else moves. Surrounding mountains stand sharp against a cloudless sky where a burning sun hangs. A few hundred metres below to the lee side of a ridge grows a humped cushion of vegetable sheep. On every side are piles of broken greywacke heaped at the bottom of the mountain faces. Only a careful search reveals an occasional plant growing amongst the debris. We begin to walk back down the mountain.

As we descend a scree slope, small landslides rattle down beside us until at last the ground firms and small plants begin to dot the surface. The stream which has disappeared under the rock debris emerges again, ice cold, in a gully. Tongues of tussock cling to the ridges which stretch up into the rock strewn slopes. Amongst the tussock and on the firmer ground low-growing plants hug the surface. As we drop into a tussock basin we hear a cicada chirping, the first animal sound for several hours. There are many plants now; spaniard flower stalks thrust above the tussock, edelweiss and gentians crown a rocky outcrop, ourisias and eyebrights shelter below the tussock. Grasshoppers, thousands of them, are feeding on the alpine vegetation and spring from the foliage as we pass.

The sweet smell of vegetation hangs in the air as we enter a narrow band of scrub which rims a shallow tarn. A black backed gull wheels high over the valley as we disappear into the upper limits of the beech forest.

Four months from now the alpine lands will be deep in snow. The stream still gurgles down the mountain but its splashing is muffled by the snow which covers most of its length. The adult insects are dead; flies frozen deep in the snow. The plants, many completely buried, others barely emerging from the snow, await spring thaw when the buds can burst and the growing season starts again. A pipit hops about a snow drift. A kea calls from the shelter of the forest below. Its strident call quickly lost on the wind which hustles snow clouds towards the mountain. The clouds scudding across the upper faces thicken and in a short time it begins to snow; gently at first. Snow and cloud merge. The pipit goes back in the forest, the wind increases until it whines around the high ridges and it is no longer possible to distinguish earth from sky. When the storm is over, four days have passed, powder snow blankets the ground in the forest. Snow is piled high on the beech branches and their dark green leaves are dusted white.

Mount Earnslaw — *Ourisia sp.*
There are some 24 known species of
Ourisia *found throughout New Zealand,*
South America and Tasmania. The ten
New Zealand species which are endemic
are found mostly in sub-alpine situations.
Some hybridism does occur between
species in the wild but in general they
remain fairly distinct.

New Zealand Eyebright — *Euphrasia*
cuneata
This plant which flowers abundantly from
January to March is found from sea level
to the alpine regions but may be common
in open sub-alpine or amongst red tussock.
It belongs to a group of plants, most of
which are root parasites. This species was
considered by Dr L. Cockayne, the well
known ecologist, to be partly parasitic,
living attached to the roots of grasses. It
occurs in open rocky places, and stream
sides although there is great variation in
the size of plants depending on where they
grow. The genus is widespread in the
temperate regions of both hemispheres.
The 15 New Zealand species are endemic.

Parahebe hookeriana
Two varieties of this plant are found, one
in the mountains of the volcanic plateau
and the other in the Ruahine range. Both
are absent from Mount Egmont. It grows
on rocky sites, especially exposed ridges,
in a variety of alpine and sub-alpine
situations. There are eleven species of
Parahebe *in New Zealand.*

Vegetable sheep — *Raoulia rubra*
Barely 6 cm high, this photograph shows the true structure of the vegetable sheep. When completely intact, the plants form a tight cushion which has the resilient feel of firm rubber. The stems branch again and again and at their extremities are covered with small tightly packed woolly leaves. The tight mass of stems and leaves forms the cushion. Within the plant is a peat formed from the rotting branches and leaves and this holds water like a sponge. Rootlets penetrate the peat to nourish the plant while the main root serves chiefly to secure it. There are 20 New Zealand species of Raoulia, 15 of which reach the alpine zone where they grow on rock outcrops or colonise stony debris in fellfield. Not all Raoulia species grow into the rounded masses known as vegetable sheep. This species is found in the Tararua Range and the mountains of north west Nelson in both low and high alpine situations.

Fellfield and scree

Fellfield occurs in high mountain areas, has very little soil, and a very light plant cover. In winter, snow may lie deep on the ground while during the summer months water drains away and warm winds combined with hot sunlight heat the slopes. Plants are continually exposed to frost except in winter when they are buried in snow and often frozen stiff at night. The growing season is short and the water that bathes their roots icy cold. Rocks litter the fellfield but they are stable enough to allow plants to grow in their shelter. Fellfield plants are mostly low growing mats, bear small leaves and in some cases no leaves at all. It is the relative stability of the rocks which distinguishes fellfield from scree slopes.

Although scree plants have to withstand some of the same conditions as fellfield plants, there are some important additional factors. Scree slopes are far less stable, the surface 10-20cm, moving most often during very wet weather or after snowfalls. Contrasting with fellfield, most screes have a permanently moist soil below the rock surface. It is in this soil that the scree plants root while the upper portion of the plant only copes with the constantly moving surface. In this way only the flowers and leafy parts of the plants are exposed. If these parts are destroyed, the plants can recover because the main resources are stored in the roots, stems and buds protected in the soil below. Additionally, although the drying winds draw moisture from the leaves, there is a constant supply of water from the soil to compensate. The plants are scattered far apart and seldom found on any site other than scree. They include Haast's buttercup — *Ranunculus haastii*, the penwiper plant — *Notothlapsi rosulatum*, scree chickweed — *Stellaria roughii*, scree bidi-bidi — *Acaena glabra*, black cotula — *Cotula atrata* and the scree Epilobium — *Epilobium pycnostachynum*.

Vegetable Sheep — *Haastia pulvinaris*
Found on rocks in the drier mountains of Nelson and Marlborough, this plant produces flowers in great numbers all over the cushion from December to January. This genus is endemic to New Zealand, all three species, each with a variety, confined to the South Island. The woody bases are completely covered by tightly packed foliage and the cushions up to 2m across are 30cms or more thick. It is the largest of the vegetable sheep and is actually a shrub complete with trunk, branchlets and leaves, superbly adapted to mountain conditions.

Phyllachne colensoi
This cushion plant occurs in the North, South and Stewart Islands in the higher montane and sub-alpine regions growing in herbfield, fellfield, rocky places, herb moor, overlying peat and short open tussock. There are three New Zealand species in the small genus which has other members in Tasmania and South America. All the plants form hard cushions or matlike masses.

Epilobium macropus
There are 50 recognised species and a number of varieties in New Zealand and some 200 species throughout the world, mainly in the temperate regions. This plant grows in permanently damp places throughout the sub-alpine regions of both main islands.

Dracophyllum muscoides
Confined to the lower parts of the South Island on boggy ground in higher montane and sub-alpine herbfield, this smallest Dracophyllum *in New Zealand is usually the most important member of cushion vegetation.*

Summer in the Travers Valley — Nelson Lakes National Park

selected references

H. H. Allan — 'Flora of New Zealand', printed by R. E. Owen, Government Printer 1970.

K. W. Allison and John Child — 'The Mosses of New Zealand', printed by University of Otago Press Dunedin 1971.

I. A. E. Atkinson — 'Check List of Indigenous Vascular Plants Recorded from Tongariro National Park' second edition approximately 1971.

I. A. E. Atkinson and B. D. Bell — Offshore and Outlying Islands 1967.

Alfred M. Bailey — 'Birds of New Zealand', published by Denver Museum of Natural History 1955.

C. M. M. Clarke — 'Flowering Periods of Alpine Plants at Cupola Basin, Nelson, New Zealand', reprinted from the New Zealand Journal of Botany, Vol. 6 No. 2 June 1968.

L. Cockayne, CMG, FRS — 'New Zealand Plants and their Story', Fourth Edition edited by E. J. Godley, printed by R. E. Owens, Government Printer 1967.

L. Cockayne, CMG, FRS — 'Vegetation of New Zealand', second edition 1928.

L. Cockayne, CMG, FRS — 'The Cultivation of New Zealand Plants', printed by Whitcombe & Tombs Ltd 1923.

L. Cockayne, CMG, PhD, FRS, FLS and E. Phillips Turner FRGS — 'The Trees of New Zealand', printed by R. E. Owens, Government Printer 1950.

M. B. Dobbie — 'New Zealand Ferns', revised and edited with additional matter by Marguerite Crookes MA, fourth edition, printed by Whitcombe & Tombs Ltd.

A. P. Druce — 'Botanical Survey of an Experimental Catchment, Taita, New Zealand', printed by Whitcombe & Tombs Ltd 1957.

R. A. Forster & L. M. Forster — 'New Zealand Spiders' an introduction, printed by Collins Bros. & Co. Ltd. 1973.

R. A. Falla, R. B. Sibson & E. G. Turbott — 'A Field Guide to the Birds of New Zealand and Outlying Islands', published by Collins Bros. & Co. Ltd. 1966.

D. R. Gregg — 'Volcanoes of Tongariro National Park', a New Zealand Geographical Survey Handbook, information series No. 28, printed by New Zealand Department of Scientific and Industrial Research, second impression 1961.

G. V. Hudson FRES, FNZ Inst. — 'New Zealand Beetles and their Larvae', printed by Ferguson & Osborn Ltd, NZ 1934.

G. V. Hudson FRES, FNZ Inst.n — 'Fragments of New Zealand Entomology', printed by Ferguson & Osborn Ltd. NZ 1950.

The Natural History of Canterbury — Edited by **G. A. Knox,** printed by A. H. & A. W. Reed Ltd. 1969.

R. M. Laing and E. W. Blackwell — 'Plants of New Zealand', printed by Whitcombe & Tombs Ltd, sixth edition 1957.

Margaret E. Lancaster — 'Forest Fungi', printed by R. E. Owens, Government Printer 1955.

A. F. Mark and Nancy M. Adams — 'New Zealand Alpine Plants', published by A. H. & A. W. Reed Ltd. 1973.

William Martin and John Child — 'Lichens of New Zealand', published by A. H. & A. W. Reed Ltd 1972.

A. H. McLintock — 'A Descriptive Atlas of New Zealand', printed by R. E. Owens, Government Printer 1959.

David Miller CBE, CMZS, FRSNZ, FRES, MSc, PhD — 'Common Insects in New Zealand', printed by A. H. & A. W. Reed Ltd 1971.

Lucy B. Moore and Nancy M. Adams — 'Plants of the New Zealand Coast', printed by Paul's Book Arcade, Auckland and Hamilton 1963.

Lucy B. Moore and Elizabeth Edgar — 'Flora of New Zealand' Volume 2, printed by A. R. Shearer, Government Printer 1970.

John Morton and Michael Miller — 'The New Zealand Sea Shore', printed by Collins Bros & Co Ltd 1968.

Notornis — Quarterly Bulletin of the Ornithological Society of New Zealand, Vols. 8-21.

W. R. B. Oliver — 'New Zealand Birds', second edition, printed by A. H. & A. W. Reed Ltd. 1955.

W. R. B. Oliver — 'The Genus Coprosma', Bernice P. Bishop Museum Bulletin No 132, published by the Museum 1935.

Ornithological Society of New Zealand Inc — 'Annotated Checklist of the Birds of New Zealand', published by A. H. & A. W. Reed Ltd 1970.

J. G. Pendergast MSc, PhD and **D. R. Cowley** MSc — 'An Introduction to New Zealand Freshwater Insects', published by Collins Bros & Co. Ltd 1966.

W. R. Philipson and D. Hearn — 'Rock Garden Plants of the Southern Alps', published by the Caxton Press, Christchurch 1962.

A. W. B. Powell — 'Shells of New Zealand', printed by Whitcombe & Tombs Ltd, third edition 1957.

J. T. Salmon — 'New Zealand Flowers and Plants in Colour', published by A. H. & A. W. Reed Ltd.

John T. Salmon DSc, FRSNZ, FRPS, — 'Field Guide to the Alpine Plants of New Zealand', printed by A. H. & A. W. Reed Ltd 1968.

Richard Sharell — 'The Tuatara, Lizards and Frogs of New Zealand', printed by Collins Bros, & Co Ltd 1966.

G. Marie Taylor nee Bulmer, — Victoria University of Wellington — 'A Key to the Coprosmas of New Zealand', Part 1 & 2, reprinted from 'Tuatara' Vol 1 No 1 Pages 31-42 September 1961.

G. Marie Taylor — 'Mushrooms and Toadstools in New Zealand', printed by A. H. & A. W. Reed Ltd 1970.

Wellington Botanical Society Bulletin No. 37, — published by Wellington Botanical Society Inc. 1971.

Wellington Botanical Society Bulletin No. 38 — published by Wellington Botanical Society Inc. 1974.

Gordon R. Williams, Editor — 'The Natural History of New Zealand', An Ecological Survey, printed by A. H. & A. W. Reed Ltd 1973.